DON'T TELL ME

I CAN'T DO IT!

JIM GRIFFITHS

ISBN-13: 978-0692154120

ISBN-10: 0692154124

DEDICATION

Through his book, a friend helped me understand something that was holding me back. The book is "Getting Unstuck," by Ron Frost.

Most people have an obstacle they are unaware of, usually from their distant past, preventing them from going beyond their current position in life. It's usually something they do or believe without realizing its existence.

They're "stuck."

When my wife and I first met I was stuck. Childhood experiences caused me to be scared of connecting with another person. Her gift to me was the strength to understand and face what was holding me back, and her patience opened my eyes to a world I may have never known.

Nothing I would have done alone could match the significance our relationship has created in my life.

Robin, I love you.

.

CONTENTS

FOREWORD

In the movie "Contact" Jodie Foster played a scientist who listened to outer space and received a digital message. The signal resulted in thousands of pages of data that didn't make sense. Someone on her team layered all of the pages, made them transparent, and saw something in each. This discovery was a code explaining the data.

As I watched that scene I thought about entrepreneurism and its multiple layers. People hear the word "entrepreneur" and automatically think about business. If you extract business from entrepreneurism you'll find secrets to achieving unmatched by any educational system.

In my early teens I ran away from home and quit school. The original plan was to get a job and do my best to stay out of jail. I got distracted by associating with people that knew how to win and found myself in a position to quit what America defines as "working" at a fairly young age. I had no family money, I didn't break any laws, and I didn't win anything. I studied what people consider the "traits of an entrepreneur" and I adopted their habits.

There's no shortage of seminars, books, classes, and other forms of education on the concept of "success principles." I've studied many, including people who have benefited by adopting them, and found similar traits specifically among entrepreneurs. I invite you to look deeper at how they face challenges, how they grow and expand ideas, and how they're often socially unaccepted because of their goals or how they think and see the world.

The entrepreneur is a problem solver that avoids the "herd" and anything else that blocks their visions. How do they maintain energy against odds or under pressure, and why are they always looking for a better way to do something? How do they stay focused under emotional pressure, or break barriers others couldn't pass through?

Historically, business ownership has been considered an American Dream, but being an entrepreneur takes things a step further. Habits, character, and behaviors separate business owners from entrepreneurs. They're architects of the future, and the world could use a few more.

The inspiration for writing the chapters of my life was stimulated by volunteering in high school business classes. Younger people confided in me as I listened to how they were nervous about entering the world of political corruption and corporate greed being handed down to them. As I connected with younger people I began to understand the gap between traditional education and what happens in the real world. That gap is not only getting wider, but deeper too. I had a front row seat to how kids are learning WHAT to think, but not HOW to. I saw kids pass that never even turned in their work, because if they didn't, the teacher was blamed and could be at risk of losing their job. I noticed how teachers care and want to do the right thing, and I also saw how a career in our educational system has become more about politics than teaching.

The down-side for younger people is they're led to believe once they get out of college all their problems will end. They get a degree, work a few years, and realize they never learned how to win. They did everything they were told to do, so why isn't it working?

The answer is because they're playing an old game with new rules.

If retiring one day is the goal, people should understand it's not a function of age. It's the result of developing an income that no longer requires your time to maintain. In the past this was done by dedicating a percentage of your life to a career. Today it will take more than working a job for thirty years to develop a retirement you can afford to live on. The days of working and collecting a reasonable retirement are not gone, but we can all agree they're not as common as they were a few decades ago.

Getting ahead today requires more than showing up to occupy a position at a company. We must individually learn to be problem solvers.

Many people wake up thinking their challenges would go away if they lived in a different city, if they were friends with someone else, or if their favored candidate won the Presidency. It's not the President's fault you don't have clearly defined goals with a date on them. It's not your friend's fault you don't identify your own bad habits, break them, and create new ones. And your current residential zip code will not change whether or not you learn from mistakes. These excuses point to blame, and even if your blame is accurate, it changes nothing. It does, however, cause people to be bitter without realizing why, which we're seeing a lot of in society.

Consider addressing the one thing people spend their life avoiding, and one of the most powerful actions known to humans; change. Most opt to keep doing exactly what they're doing and hope for the best. Perhaps someone will leave a big box of money on your front porch. Unfortunately, turning a blind eye and living in denial is an inevitable dead end. You'll find yourself to be one that says, "I'm doing okay" or "I'm getting by," yet that status was never your goal.

Ultimately, I see people to be in search of the same elements that make up a full life; a combination of time, money, and a feeling of significance. If you set a course to balance those three, you'll find everything else to revolve around them. Significance seems to be the neglected element. Most people are way out of balance with a strong focus on making money first, then complain they have no time to develop something significant. I found successful people to be after the same three magic things, with a different order of priority. They focus efforts on what will develop into something significant, which money becomes a reflection of, ultimately creating time.

My ten dollars and my ten minutes is equal to yours. Significance, on the other hand, is different for everyone. I found significance in helping people learn from my failures, my successes, and my mistakes. Who'd of thought to look there? Once I shared how I went from a small business owner to adopting an entrepreneur's mentality, and made that information available to other people, it became profitable. Time became a byproduct, creating even more significance. It didn't start with trying to make a buck, it started by offering something of value, which was sharing information that could help others. And round and round we go.

People who have done it would agree; most personal enterprises were built in a year. It may have taken twenty years to get started, and it may take twenty more to evolve, but that first year of commitment sets a foundation that makes everything else happen. The challenge; are you willing to put your hobbies and toys on hold, adopt the traits of an entrepreneur, and incorporate their habits into all facets of your life?

CHAPTER ONE

DON'T TELL ME I CAN'T DO IT!

I credit most of my life's successes to an experience I had when I was a kid in Key Largo. It was the first time I can remember being fueled by someone telling me I couldn't do something. I've wondered why they would say it, and if they were right. I often catch myself doing something only because someone said I couldn't. I even catch myself doing things just to see if I can. This has created a lot of wins in my life and I'm grateful it has become a habit.

We moved around a lot when I was young. My parents were not together, and I lived with my father because there were less rules. My dad's career path was law enforcement and he changed jobs a lot. When I was around ten years old he got a job with the Florida State Marine Patrol that moved us to the upper end of the Florida Keys. This was an exciting time to be a police officer on the water in the Keys. It was in the late seventies and we had a front-row seat to the biggest drug smuggling movement the area has ever seen. Yes, he saw a lot of that action.

I was not excited about moving at first. We had moved several times over the last few years. I had new friends at a new school, and I was once again THAT kid, the one who walked into a new classroom not knowing anyone. But living in a home on the water in Key Largo changed all of that.

We all love what we're good at. I found something I loved, and something I was great at. It was fishing. My first encounter off the seawall was with a school of fish called Snappers, and it didn't take long to find out the big ones were rarely caught. Establishing a plan to catch one of the bigger fish was the first time I can remember thinking like an entrepreneur. I had a goal, I was motivated, I created a plan, and I executed it. My first attempt at catching what a kid would consider a monster didn't go so well. This wasn't going to be easy. The bigger ones were smarter than I thought they'd be.

I wanted to get fish in the habit of coming to my dock, so part of the catch-plan was to get the neighborhood fish accustomed to food regularly being served at my home. Every afternoon I would throw scraps into the water, and soon it was almost as if the fish knew what time I got home from school.

Key Largo's clear waters in the seventies was like looking into an aquarium. Sometimes as a school of Snappers swam by I would throw several scraps of bait into the water to observe their habits. During the first few days the splash of bait hitting the water scared them away. Eventually it was more of a dinner-bell and that same splash turned out to be what attracted them. I got the fish so caught up in the excitement of eating that they didn't notice me on the dock trying to catch them.

I needed to work on tactics and ideas, and one was to throw a few scraps of bait in the water to attract them, while one of the baits secretly had a hook in it. I really thought I was being clever. The feeding frenzy began before the bait could even sink, and within a few seconds it was all gone, except for the bait with my hook in it. It would just lay there on the bottom a few feet below the surface. The school of fish swam around that one lonely bait for a few minutes. They got close and looked at it, but wouldn't eat it. Eventually a small fish took his chances and became part of my catch, but I didn't want a small one. Anyone could catch a small one.

Without realizing it, the entrepreneur inside of me was starting to develop. I experienced failure, frustration, and the inability to accomplish something I had put so much effort into. This didn't make sense. It shouldn't be this hard. I felt things that most adults have felt at some point in their life. Was I no good at this? Should I just quit and just settle for smaller fish? Should I stop before anyone sees what a failure I am? Should I lie about catching a big fish so people would respect me? Should I be normal like my neighbors and just be grateful for being able to catch smaller fish?

I recall a story of a guy hitting a wall. Hitting and hitting and hitting. He gives up not knowing that the wall was crumbling on the other side. One or two more swings, and the wall would have crumbled to pebbles. He got caught up in something that stops a lot of people from accomplishing things; he couldn't physically see it. An entrepreneur has a different philosophy; instead of "I'll believe it when I see it," they think, "I'll see it when I believe it."

When people can't find solutions to a challenge, there are answers and options on the table, but sometimes they're hard to see because they're covered by things like stress or frustration. Frustration is a powerful creativity blocker. It's dangerous to a goal. However, if you know how to use it, it can be a goal's best friend. Frustration is thought of as a negative emotion, and it probably is most of the time, but emotional redirection is a valuable tactic when you learn how to incorporate it. I had a goal and I was using frustration as a fuel instead of something that would block my mind from thinking creatively.

I caught a break. I soon acquired a powerful fuel from a neighbor across the canal I was able to combine with my frustrations. Roy, a mechanic that worked at the Miami International Airport, lived forty feet across the water and had been watching me for weeks. One day he commented how he knew what I was trying to do. He attempted to educate me about their size being a reflection of how smart they were. In that case, I figured I must be smarter than any of them. The big ones were about fifteen inches while I measured at least sixty inches, making me several times larger. I figured that if size were an issue worthy of attention I'll win this one.

Roy was quite a contributor to my young and developing entrepreneurial mind. I refused to accept what people around me believed, and I refused to think that it couldn't be done. I also wasn't willing to accept the opinion of one person. Today I find this to be what prevents adults from getting many things they once wanted.

I weighed about eighty pounds and knew nothing about fishing, but I just couldn't accept that a fish swimming in a canal in Key Largo would outsmart me. It wasn't about fishing, I had a goal.

My attempts to catch a big Snapper went on for weeks. I tried everything I could think of but just couldn't figure out what would entice one of the bigger fish to bite. I did not understand how smart they were, but I remember thinking that if I could see them, they could probably see me, so I dragged a potted plant out to the dock to hide behind. I thought that was clever, but I have no proof that it fooled the fish.

Trying to catch one particular fish became an obsession. But it wasn't about a fish, it was about how I wouldn't quit till I knew I had exhausted every option. It had to be possible, but I couldn't stop wondering what the secret could be. I tried different baits, different kinds of fishing line, and even different hooks. I tried something different every afternoon. I got good at catching the small ones, but the larger ones evaded me. It was exciting, challenging, and I was hooked!

The best part of the memory, and how I've benefited from it the most, is how hard it was. If it were easy, everyone could flop a fifteen-inch fish onto the dock. But things that come easy, or things we don't have to earn, don't offer great rewards.

About a mile from my dock was a classic Keys bait shop. I rode my bike there a couple times a week to watch the owner build custom fishing rods through a glass wall that separated his work bench from the tackle shop. I was fascinated with components that made a custom fishing rod along with the whole assembly process. I was especially mesmerized with the weaving of colorful threads that made up the unique designs of each fishing rod.

Unfortunately, most adults learn something and do it the same way indefinitely, then complain about how things around them are not changing. This has always puzzled me among adults, and it's exactly what this story is about; the concept of trying different things. I watch people try to use what they know and expect different results. It never works. Add to what you know and change what you think or believe with books, videos, and seminars. Use anything you can. The part that puzzles me is how people are not happy where they end up yet they never did anything different to change it. Where did you expect to end up if you changed nothing?

Back at the bait shop I figured if this guy makes custom fishing rods, he must know how to fish. I wondered if he'd share any advice on how to catch the big ones. This, in today's world, is considered consulting, and Charlie Rowell at Rowell's Marina was my first consultant. Having a lifelong Key Largo presence in the bait and tackle industry, he knew of tactics I would never have thought of on my own.

There's a lot of power in involving other minds. When considering a consultant, extensive experience is a big help but not a requirement for me. I look for someone willing to open their mind and think with me. I look for someone that leaves excuses at the door, and someone that shares a personal belief with me; the belief that there's always a way.

Collect as much information from other people you can. People think different, and they all bring something to the table. You can learn as much from the town idiot as you can from a college graduate if you're listening. Today I consider the concept of consulting a must in entrepreneurism, and something Charlie brought to my attention was about to pay off.

Charlie was intrigued with an inquisitive youngster and admired my ambition. He put his work aside for a few minutes and invited me out to his fuel docks on the bay where a lot of Snappers gathered because of the overflow from his dockside bait tanks. Into the water went a handful of bait scraps to observe how the fish behaved. We noticed a trend. A smaller fish would often grab a large bait and quickly attempt to escape with it, but a bigger fish would eventually swoop in and take it away. We had stumbled across what would eventually be the secret to catching a big dockside Snapper in Key Largo.

I envisioning the mayor giving me a key to the city and a erecting a bronze statue honoring my historical success for tourists as they cross bridges leading into the Florida Keys.

Months of persistence were about to pay off. The long-awaited solution was to put several scraps of bait where there were no fish and hide my hook in the biggest one. I would then let it all lay together on the bottom, lean back out of sight, and wait. As fish made their rounds up and down the neighborhood's seawall, they picked up on the scent and a feeding frenzy took place. A smaller fish grabbed my oversized bait and attempted a getaway. The biggest fish in the school spotted the little fish trying to make his escape and swooped in to take the bait away from the smaller fish, which ended up being the one with my hook in it.

This makes me think of what has been recently branded as "fake news." It's easy to get caught up in the commotion of an exciting or dynamic news story then we hear about another one so quickly that we never really knew the facts of the last one. This is a media tactic to keep you on the edge of your seat which drives ratings to stimulate advertising dollars.

I see this as one of America's greatest challenges; we are moving so quickly we don't have time to gather facts. This causes bad decisions, then the inevitable domino effect of more inaccurate information and more bad decisions follow. It's an interesting circle, and it's why I don't watch TV or read newspapers. I'd prefer to be uninformed than misinformed. If we're going into a recession, or if a hurricane is coming, or if we're going to war, I'll find out about it. He rest seems to be drama and "fluff" to sell advertising. I turned off my TV years ago and find myself to be more factually informed without it.

The technique I learned from Charlie Rowell soon put a fifteen-inch Snapper on the dock which was about as big as they got in that canal. As far as I know, it was the first fish that size the neighborhood had ever seen out of the water. Success! Now that I knew the trick, I was consistently catching big Snappers every afternoon. It worked every time.

This reminds me of my life today. People think I have a magic wand just as neighbors thought I was lucky every time I fished. It wasn't luck, and they wouldn't have used that word had they known what I went through to develop the skills. My peers often claim everything I touch turns to gold. Lucky for me, they haven't seen quite everything I've touched. I've got a lot more failures than successes. I once told a group of high school kids that if I had a nickel for every time I succeeded, I wouldn't have as many nickels had I collected one for every time I failed.

This story is not about fishing. It's about consistently trying something different, improving technique, and learning from your mistakes. It's about not giving up, and though I landed a big fish there was still one more thing to do.

Roy across the canal came home from work at exactly 6:25 daily and he could see my backyard from where he parked his truck. At 6PM sharp I started "chumming" the water to attract fish. Not too much. I used minced up teaser-baits because I didn't want the fish to get full and leave. When Roy pulled into his driveway, I put my proven technique to work. I threw assorted pieces of bait into the water with my hook in the largest one. By the time Roy gathered his things and made his way to his front door he heard whooping and hollering as I tossed a whopper on the dock. I said, "Hey Roy, look what I just caught!"

Roy said something that I still hear today when I do things others can't figure out how to do. He said, "You got lucky." What a thing to tell a kid that worked so hard for so long, but I knew deep down I earned the reward of that catch. He also commented about how anyone could catch one. He asked if I could do it again. I didn't have the heart to tell him I had caught several over the last few days.

There are a lot of valuable entrepreneurial lessons in this story. A big one is to admire the accomplishment, but get back to work. Figuring out how to do something is great, but quickly going back to work creates the habit of winning through momentum. If a baseball player sends a fastball to the fence and stands there to admire his swing for too long, his odds at making it around the bases drops by the millisecond. A quick glance at your success will offer excitement, which can help produce adrenaline that will increase your speed around the bases, but focus on taking the next step.

Success, in the baseball player's case, is not the hit; it's how far they can successfully make it around the bases. For me, the success was not only if I could catch one big fish, it was if I could catch another. A second would decrease the thought of it being credited to luck. As far as the next step, mine was to take a shot at the Tarpon, a much larger and prized fish that swam in our canals at night. This was another thing neighbors claimed to have never been done…. but I did that too.

Think hard about that baseball player analogy. So many get caught up in how hard they can hit the ball, yet hitting the ball is not the goal. Making it to home plate is the goal.

An entrepreneur is not bulletproof, but they also don't let distractions or negative neighbors win. There's an old saying about not letting people get your goat. They can't if you don't tell them where you left it. Let no one get the best of you or decide if you win or lose. Make that a reflection of your choices.

The memory of Roy, who I consider my first critic, was an inspirational lesson that has served me well ever since. I've crossed paths with others like him and they all remind me of why some people accomplish new things, and why some don't. From that day forward the word "luck" has meant something unique to me. I believe in luck, it has its place and I'll take it when I can. But I don't depend on it.

Those fish were not defeated with luck, they were earned through trial and error. Lots of errors! Instead of accepting that it couldn't be done, I worked hard, I was persistent, and I applied different tactics. I was able to block out distractions and temporary failures that stop most people from doing what I did. I applied weeks of creative efforts and I won. I felt like I accomplished something and wondered why the neighbor had been encouraging me to give up or quit. Was he scared that he may look bad if a kid did something he couldn't do?

We all choose who we associate with, and I believe in the philosophy of becoming what and who we're around. Do you associate with people that breathe life into you, or do you stand by as they suck it out?

In my home office I have a photo of a Mangrove Snapper on the wall, along with many things that keep other memories in front of me. That photo is a reminder about how people credit luck with accomplishments. It visually reminds me to work hard and consistently try new tactics.

Don't be so quick to give up. Breaking routine and going from good to great is about learning how to figure things out. It's about not accepting average and always working towards making something better. Make getting better a habit, and people will soon think you too have a magic wand that turns everything you touch into gold.

As far as I know not one person on that canal in Key Largo ever caught one of the larger snappers, and I'd bet every one of those people fished the same technique every time. Does that sound familiar in society? People think collecting certificates and degrees will solve everything. A college degree didn't catch that fish, and it didn't take thousands of dollars. Fishing school can teach you how to tie knots, how to test the line strength, and maybe the science of how to fish the tides and moons, but it doesn't teach what it took to catch that fish.

I support school and encourage advanced learning centers like colleges and tech schools, but I also believe the knowledge needs to be combined with lessons hidden within the layers of entrepreneurism if you truly want to separate yourself from the masses and create successes in your personal life.

Most people have experiences like this, not only from their childhood, but from last week as well. We're always experiencing. The question is more about if we're learning from those experiences, using them to improve, or do we just take pictures and call them experiences and/or memories? People that experience without learning are the ones that end up in the same place every few years.

Think about those big Snappers the next time you think about getting anything you want out of life. If you want it bad enough, there's a way. Figure it out. Practice getting better at something even if it doesn't need to be better. That practice will come in handy for when you need it.

Charlie Rowell was intrigued with my persistence at such a young age. We soon befriended each other, and he allowed me behind the counter after school to get a close-up view of how custom fishing rods were made. I'm sure he was eventually more cautious as to who he showed his talents to because I became a competitor within a few months. He didn't mind, he invited the competition and offered to outsource his repair jobs to me since he was so booked with custom rod orders.

It was the late seventies and I had my first business, Jimmy's Rod Shop, Key Largo, Florida. If you want to reach someone, you have to build trust. Charlie trusted me and is forever on my personal list of people that helped me build character and believe in myself at a young age.

I'll feel guilty leaving you hanging without at least one story from my dad's police days in the Upper Keys. I was in my early teens and working at the boat rental docks at Pennekamp State Park in Key Largo. It was a weekend morning and I was getting all the boats started and ready for the day's rentals. Out of nowhere a cop jumped into what was once a drug dealer's boat, a forty-five-foot Cigarette racing boat with a new blue-light on it, and went racing out of the marina at max speed. A couple hours later we found out why.

My dad was on his way from our house to Pennekamp for his morning coffee and spotted a commercial fishing boat stuck in shallow water. He approached to assist and could smell marijuana as he got closer. The crew knew they had nowhere to go and no choice but to be arrested. As my dad escorted them on to his patrol boat, one shoved him into the water and they stole his boat. They attempted to run him over, but dad was able to stay safe by dodging under the hull of their fishing boat.

He emptied his revolver in their direction, and they were out of sight in seconds. The boat ended up being found in mangroves later that day. Lucky for my dad, a woman having coffee on her porch overlooking Largo Sound saw the whole thing and called the police. The smugglers were long gone, but their boat was towed to the boat rental docks where I worked.

US Customs unloaded more than three-hundred bails of marijuana from the boat onto the docks at Pennekamp Park. It was my dad's biggest bust, till a couple years later when he seized an RV with dozens of Army duffle bags full of cocaine, which was the largest cocaine bust in US history at the time. This landed him an interview in the TV series "Cocaine Cowboys."

Working at the park was nonstop fun and excitement. I wish I had taken more pictures and kept a journal. One day a morning snorkel boat tour was canceled and I saw the crew run down the dock to jump in a rental boat. They raced out to Molasses Reef just off Key Largo where the glass bottom boat was headed, getting there about a half hour prior. The guys had scuba gear, beach chairs, and waterproof books that people used for fish and coral identification. A plan was coordinated with the captain of the glass bottom boat to drift over them as they were lying in their beach chairs reading their books.

As the glass bottom boat got close in about thirty feet of water at the reef, the divers took a deep breath and stashed their dive mask and scuba tanks under the chairs as the glass bottom boat floated by. Tourists didn't quite know what to think about seeing two guys underwater thirty feet down reading books in a beach chair. Antics like this as a kid made it exciting to live in the Florida Keys.

My dad ended up getting fired from almost every job he had. He just never could adjust to the system. My sister died young from breast cancer and dad showed up for her funeral, but I never saw him after that. He just disappeared into society.

I credit my dad for a lot of what I figured out about life. He never wanted kids and I don't hold that against him. I was never abused, I wasn't beaten, and he never criticized or insulted me. He never even claimed that I wouldn't amount to anything or put me down in any way I can remember.

He was a cop. And as I think like an entrepreneur, he thought like a cop. Once I slipped out of town to visit my mom because of an argument I was having with my dad. The car was mine but registered in his name, so when I returned he added Grand Theft Auto to my juvenile record.

Officers in his command brought me soda and candy bars while I was in jail. He was a Sergeant and they didn't seem to like working for him. He was not only a cop as a career but personally as well. My time in the "Big House" only lasted a few hours, and though I was pretty upset at the time, I didn't hold this against him long term. He never knew how to act or communicate as a father. His idea of punishment for what I did was arrest. He did what he knew how to, as we all do.

Of all the things my father didn't do, he did teach me what NOT to do based on mistakes he made, and that was a lot more than what many dads do for their kids.

For years I harbored feelings of blame. I blamed him for everything that bothered me from my sister's cancer to my low self-esteem earlier in life, and even my mother's suicide years after they had even spoken. When I started to see how he may have been to blame for some of my past but I was responsible for my future, things started to change. In many ways I actually credit our relationship to successes. I was put into "survival" mode at an early age and learned how to make things happen or I suffered.

How many people are out there looking for a magic pill or hoping they'll get lucky one day? Many times I'd rather be lucky than good, but luck can't be consistently depended on and in a way it's the opposite of making things happen.

Whatever it takes, I encourage people to learn how to make things happen. The shortcut is studying the habits and traits of an entrepreneur.

Remember the phrase, "The harder I work, the luckier I get."

JIM GRIFFITHS

CHAPTER TWO

JIMMY'S ROD SHOP

My first business making custom fishing rods became a passion. I was now about thirteen and after learning the basics from Charlie Rowell I decided to attempt making one of my own rods from scratch. I needed practice, so with a kitchen knife I stripped the guides off one of my dad's fishing rods and tried to re-wrap them using household thread.

I brought the finished product to Charlie Rowell for inspection. The threads were far from even and I used my sister's nail polish to seal them. Needless to say, my work didn't pass inspection. But Charlie, being the unique character he was, showed me the proper way to wrap guides onto a rod and sent me back home for attempt number two. I passed inspection and was in the custom rod business.

My first order for a custom made fishing rod was from Howard Curtis, my boss and mentor at the boat rentals at Pennekamp Park. He wanted a short stout rod with a big reel on it for "Schoolie Dolphin" fishing. It was a rod you couldn't find in a store. Charlie Rowell was happy to sell me the parts and a few days later I delivered my first custom rod. Thirteen years old and in my own business!

When I was old enough to drive I still worked on the docks at Pennekamp Park boat rentals, and I also worked at the Ocean Reef Club, a private club on the northern tip of Key Largo. A lot of celebrities passed through, but staff was not allowed to talk to or associate with guests. A quick hello to some of them would have been worth getting fired over. I worked in the club's tackle shop, and I would occasionally substitute as a first-mate on some of the charter fishing boats.

Howard Curtis, my first boss, taught me a countless amount of what it takes to make things happen in the real world. He would stop in everyday just before noon, go to lunch with his friends at the park, and then go home for a nap. That was his work schedule, and he was who I wanted to be when I grew up.

One Friday he showed up with paychecks, as he always did on Fridays, but this time he personally handed over my envelope with a comment. The comment was that if I share this with coworkers, I wouldn't be working here anymore.

I opened my envelope to find I was now making more money per hour than he was paying our mechanics. I had to know why. If I could find out why I could do it again and make even more. I inquired in private and he explained how my work habits were equal to him having two kids working the docks. Mathematically, he and I both were coming out ahead by paying me more, as opposed to hiring a second person.

Other kids worked there and didn't like their job. I didn't see it as a job, I saw it as entrepreneur training by observing Howard's business decisions. This is an example as to how education is all around us.

On weekends he assigned a minimal staff while weekdays we had three or four people working. This made little sense to me, but I knew that he always had a good reason for things he did. His thinking in this case was that on weekends we had tourists renting boats. All we had to do was get them in the boats, then clean and fuel the boats for the next day. During the week, however, was when we needed staff. That's when we scheduled repairs and maintenance. If every boat was not in working order come Saturday morning, we lost money. I learned a lot from this guy.

Many days off were spent watching tourists launch boats. Park rangers shared weekend standby duty at the ramp with a tractor for those who forgot to set their emergency brake..... Trucks don't float!

I never got to say goodbye to Howard. Later in life I tried to track him down to thank him for reaching out to a young teen with an attitude problem, and for the valuable life-lessons I got from a job on a dock. I located his wife on a farm the couple bought when they sold the boat rental business. He died of lung cancer just a few months prior.

Rest in peace Howard. Your willingness to mentor a young scared kid continues to make a difference.

CHAPTER THREE

EVERYTHING'S A-OK

After quitting school in my mid-teens I landed in Homestead, a city just before you enter the Florida Keys. My thread weaving skills had improved and my custom rods were in demand by local fishermen, so I started to peddle them at local bait shops.

I was showing off my work to Johnny Fine, the owner of A-OK Bait and Tackle, when he asked where my shop was. I pointed at the fifteen-year-old rusted El Camino outside of his front door. I was living with friends at the time and didn't have a shop to work in. I wrapped rods using a wooden stand I made which sat in the back of my El Camino as I did my work in the shade under an oak tree.

Johnny didn't know what to think of me, but he did recognize entrepreneurial characteristics, and one entrepreneur is naturally attracted to another. Johnny saw talent and my willingness to work, and that attractive combination led to a great working relationship, and a great friend. Johnny walked me through the shop to a storage room. I was instructed to move everything to the left side of the room. I moved this and that, and set up a table in the corner, and poof, there was Jimmy's Rod Shop.

I worked retail in the store part-time and made rods in their storage room. We had a great working relationship, and Johnny made his way onto my list of people that gave me a chance. He asked two things of me; a ten-dollar commission per rod sold, and he wanted me to promise I would do more with my life than work in a bait shop.

Johnny was a mentor, though he never meant to be a teacher or wanted another kid. Every day he came up with unique ideas that made his business run more efficient. He was the most creative person I've ever been around. He'd walk around the shop several times a day and stare at things. While new employees thought he was having "senior moments," he was actually thinking of ways to make a part of the business run better. What he was looking for was the shop's next weakest link.

A-OK Bait & Tackle sold ten to twelve-thousand bait shrimp on a Saturday morning while other shops called two-thousand a good day. The business needed his talents to make all of this work. He created his own system for things we did a lot, like counting shrimp and bagging ice. His ideas cut labor time into fractions compared to how traditional businesses ran. He was gifted when it came to finding ways to do things better. He was a true entrepreneur.

The store attracted a lot more than fishermen. Farming was big in Homestead at the time and field drivers would come in early to get blocks of ice for their water coolers. (We also sold more Igloo coolers than any store in the area.)

Our only competitor was a block over on the main road next to a gas station. They had a much larger parking lot, plus easier trailer access, and sold about three-thousand shrimp over a weekend. A-OK Bait and Tackle sold more than that during the first hour of a Saturday morning. We had boats lined down Krome Avenue and Johnny was the perfect guy to make things operate efficiently.

He saw things in his head and had a talent when it came to making ideas a reality. The ice blocks, for example, were causing a traffic jam in both the parking lot and in the store. We knew the farmers. They were local and could be trusted with an account as opposed to making their drivers pay a dollar every morning for a block of ice. We altered their form of payment from cash to accounts on a clipboard. Now they could just let us know which farm they were with, we'd mark it down, and they could get out of the way allowing us to get back to selling bait.

To take things a step further, Johnny noticed that every time someone needed a block of ice, it took staff off the floor. We needed that staff. There were people waiting for shrimp when we opened the doors at 5am, and there was more money in shrimp than in ice.

What made this guy unique was his habit of scraping the surface and looking deeper to see things others would have normally skipped past. What he was looking for was the store's needs. We were so busy that a need was to prevent customers from going to a competitor. These guys were going fishing and their start-time was a priority. They may have considered buying bait elsewhere if they had to wait because staff was busy getting a farmer a block of ice.

Traditional thinking would conclude that everyone deals with it so just let it be, or quit selling blocks of ice. Johnny was anything but traditional.

One afternoon we heard the pounding of a hammer on the outer wall of the store. It was Johnny punching a hole in the concrete wall between the walk-in freezer and the parking lot. He rigged a conveyor belt inside the walk-in freezer to a switch at the cash register. Now a farmer could stick their head in the door and yell "Davis Farms, one block" and shut the door. We triggered the switch behind the counter sending a block of ice to the outside chute, then marked down a block of ice on the clipboard for Davis Farms, and billed them monthly.

Johnny saw a need and created a solution. From the time a farmer got in line to order a block of ice till the time he got it took four to six minutes. The conveyor belt system now took less than a minute for someone to get a block of ice. What changed was how much time and attention could now be directed towards the people in line waiting for bait and tackle. Taking on one thing at a time, he made every part of that business work efficiently.

Johnny noticed bags of ice being as time consuming as blocks, so he cut a hole in the ceiling in the walk-in cooler. (He seemed to like cutting holes in the building.) Johnny installed an ice machine on the roof over the walk-in cooler, and ice now fell into a huge container on wheels. Now we could offer buckets of ice which was faster than bagging ice, and more convenient for the fishermen.

Working at that bait shop for the short time I did was like attending "Efficiency University." Watching Johnny work was an educational process our school system could use. I was most impressed with his ability to see what the next need was. I watch people work so hard trying to fix or better something without first putting effort into finding out exactly what it is that's broken. I can't think of how many times I've been in a business and saw something that was an inconvenience to the customer. Instead of it being fixed or changed, you'd hear "That's how everyone else does it."

THAT is why most people wake up in the same place twenty or thirty years from now; because they're doing things the same way that everyone else does it. Having a "that's good enough" attitude is holding a lot of businesses back, and it's holding many people back from what they once personally dreamed about.

Fishermen often returned to the bait shop from a day on the water with extra fish that could be sold, so Johnny opened a fish market on the back side of the building. Now we'd sell you bait, tackle, ice and sandwiches, and when you got back, we'd buy your fish, and sell them to someone else. There was money in every facet of the business. He actually created a way to give your money back to you after you enjoyed a day on the water.

Johnny custom created his own one-stop-shop that was a win/win for everyone involved.

I could watch him work all day long. He was by far the person I learned the most from when it came to creating a way to make something better. He never saw things as "good enough" and always focused on the next weakest link.

About a dozen other people worked there. I was the only one fascinated with how Johnny operated, and I was the only one who saw it as an entrepreneurial learning experience. Most of the other workers were too busy being miserable and complaining because they had to wake up early. They never saw the priceless learning opportunity right in front of them.

I was recently invited to talk to a local college business class about creating a competitive edge and a student asked if I thought entrepreneurial thinking is a born gift or something you could learn. I answered with a story referring to A-OK Bait & Tackle and explained how I was exposed to entrepreneurism by watching someone's work habits. So were the other workers, but I didn't just look back at it as an experience, a place I worked, or a specific time in my past. I watched, I learned, and I later applied those things to my own life.

I explained the importance of being a person who learns from experiences as opposed to just being in the room. Do that and you'll develop entrepreneurial habits without even realizing it. If you want to manage a business, study business. If you want to be an entrepreneur, study behaviors and habits or you may become a slave to "running" your business.

A-OK's run lasted more than twenty-five good years. Hurricane Andrew blew through in 1992 and not only ruined farming in the area, but it also took the roof off that old bait shop.

The building is still there, but Johnny sold the property and retired.

CHAPTER FOUR

THE ROCK STAR

As a teen in the Florida Keys I worked at a dive shop, boat rentals, I made custom fishing rods, plus worked for a carpet cleaning company. I also worked in bait shops and occasionally on charter fishing boats. Everyone in my peer group saw me getting a captain's license and one day operating a fishing boat.

The boats I worked on were not just boats, they were fishing mega-yachts, and they were not owned by their captain. They were owned by corporations and used as high-dollar company getaways. Boat captains were respected, and they made decent money, but as far as being a fishing boat captain, my dreams were more about being the one who owned the boat, not the guy hired to drive or maintain it.

On those beautiful fishing yachts we took clients to reefs about five miles off Key Largo's coast. As we headed out of the main channel I would point northeast and mention to our charter how Bimini was only seventy miles away. I'd say, "It wouldn't take long to get there. We could catch some great fish and you could take a seaplane home." Once they realized I was serious, one out of about twenty charters took advantage of the opportunity. That afternoon they would buy us dinner and return home on the next flight, leaving us with the yacht and a full tank of fuel to fish our way home. This made it tempting to get my captain's license, but my dreams were bigger than driving some else's boat.

At age seventeen I thought I wanted to be in the US Coast Guard. I joined and went to Cape May, New Jersey, where I saw snow for the first time. I got kicked out about two weeks later. Apparently I was not ready for discipline or routine, so back to the Keys I went. I was a unique case and they left me with the option to return in a year, but a Bon Jovi video caught my attention and my next dream was to be a rock star.

It was the dawn of heavy metal music which I didn't get exposed to a lot of while living in the Keys. Tourists are obviously not much into heavy metal when visiting tropical islands, so our local bands didn't play that kind of music. I was a Jimmy Buffett fan too, but Jimmy didn't have as many flashing lights and women didn't throw their clothes at him like they did at rock stars.

MTV was on fire at the time but cable had not yet come to residents of the Upper Keys. At a restaurant in Islamorada, who had cable, I saw a Bon Jovi video, the first music video I had seen. Those three minutes were all it took. I sold my rod shop, a car and a motorcycle, quit two jobs, and left the Keys a few weeks later to pursue the dream of being a rock star.

It takes a lot to pack up everything and move across the country as a teenager with no idea how you'll survive, though survival was something I was actually good at. Fear should have stopped me, but the dream of being the next Bon Jovi overpowered my fears. Recently a high school student opened my eyes to the role fear can play in your life. Thanks to Nicole's example, fear has become one of my best friends.

Nicole

I met Nicole at a weekly talk I hosted in a friend's empty office building, "The Entrepreneur's Balcony." This weekly gathering attracted thirty to forty people interested in the concept of entrepreneurial behaviors. I was the host and coordinator, but to keep it from becoming the "Jim Show" I invited guest speakers to be the star of the evening to talk about our weekly topic. A lot of the same people attended regularly and all got the opportunity to hear thoughts, philosophies, and opinions from locally successful people. It was educational and inspiring.

A young woman attended almost every week, sat in the back, remained quiet, and took a lot of notes. I knew who it was because I knew her sister. One evening she pulled me aside and explained how much she enjoyed coming to these meetings. She could see adopting the traits of an entrepreneur to have value.

The gatherings were free to the community plus a local business donated pizza and soft drinks. Nicole was in high school and explained how nothing like this exists in the school system and she wanted to come every week. She didn't drive at the time, but always found a way to the meetings. She asked if I was okay with her sitting in the back of the room and not participating with the group. She made it clear she did not want to be called upon to say anything to or ever address the group.

This sent up a red flag. Nicole had a fear most live with; addressing a live crowd. I had a hunch she was secretly asking for my help. I assured her that she'll never be called on if she didn't want to be. She showed a sign of relief till I said, "Except for next week's meeting."

She turned pale and asked what I meant by that. I explained how this gathering was about adopting traits and habits of an entrepreneur, and how part of it is facing fears. I wasn't asking her to beat or conquer any fears. I just wanted her to taste it so later in life she would understand more about how to deal with the anxiety fear causes. I told her she didn't need to put too much into it, just come up with a topic of choice and give the group a sixty second presentation. She agreed.

I thought I lost her, but a couple days later Nicole called me and said, "Sixty seconds really flies by, can I have three minutes?" I shifted gears into a new challenge. I changed it to three minutes, but also explained how I felt bad for putting her front-center like that. It could have been scary. I offered to have two or three other people do the same so the spotlight was not only on her. She was relieved, and again I had something up my sleeve. I wanted more. I asked her to write her own eulogy and read it to the class. I explained how this would be easy. She never even had to look up, just read. Again, she agreed.

The next Entrepreneur's Balcony rolled around and Nicole delivered the most impressive three-minute talk about how a kid getting a sixty percent grade and being permitted to go to the next level is not acceptable. It's a topic that had come up with our group before, but she added so much more flavor to it. People cheered, and Nicole glowed.

After others did their talks, I asked for Nicole to come back up because she had one more thing to share. Nicole read about how a woman recently died warm in her bed at the age of ninety-two. She was a writer with several novels in her collection. She traveled the world and spent a lot of time with underprivileged kids. Nicole talked about how this woman was also an in-demand public speaker and how she credited that to a fear she was encouraged to face at an early age.

People got so caught up in the tale of accomplishment and Nicole's ability to tell the story so well they didn't realize the old woman she was reading about was Nicole herself decades from now.

I'd have to admit, I got a little misty myself. She credits me for encouraging her to follow through with this, but she did the hard part. A teenage woman was willing to face what she thought was her greatest fear. Not to beat it, but just to know more about it, and ended up beating it. After that, Nicole sat up front, was the first to put her hand up, the first to volunteer, and she started writing her first book.

Different people collect and remember different things from experiences. This one offered the group a front row seat to witnessing a young person face and work through what she saw as her greatest fear. Nicole's fear was a bully that learned while it may have been strong and intimidating most of the time, and it may be accustomed to winning, it wasn't going to win this time.

The unwillingness to face a fear, or sweeping it under a rug, is one of the reasons people die with a void in their life. Facing what scares you builds character. Don't die wondering what something may have been if only you were willing to face a fear.

There's a time and a place to turn the other cheek and a time to stand up to your fears. It's not about the act of fighting back, it's about the willingness to. If you're willing to stand up to a fear once, it may win that one time, but it will not be as quick to intimidate you the next time. It now weighs less because it knows you're willing to fight back, and less weight on your back allows room for more important things.

Sacramento

Prior to Nicole teaching me about fear I landed in Sacramento, California, with short hair, a dream, and all of my possessions in one duffel bag. I rented space in an old Victorian house that had three bedrooms converted into one-room apartments. Rent was $160 a month and I shared a bathroom with two neighbors. I picked up a room-mate, Keith, which cut my monthly rental cost down to $80 a month.

Keith was the starving college student and I was the starving musician. We each had a mattress on the floor. Plastic milk crates divided them as something to keep our clothes off the floor. I was scared, but I wasn't alone, and I was excited to be chasing a dream. Call it luck or call it God, but my new friend Keith was a gift. We were both struggling to achieve something; me a rock star, and him a college degree. He and I had a unique friendship and we're still in touch today.

I got a minimum wage job at a car wash on Folsom Boulevard in Sacramento. Money was tight, but I was so excited to be chasing a dream, as long as I had rent and food, money didn't matter. Most successful musicians were once a starving musician, so it felt like I was on track. That minimum wage job didn't last long. The manager took a career offer in southern California and I was asked to fill his position. I was surprised at the offer. I had stringy hair half way down my back and was more interested in playing guitar than working, but Mr. Ben, the owner of the car wash, needed someone with honesty and integrity, and someone who was on time every day, never hung-over, and treated customers with respect. I was the guy. Something else I now had was a more substantial income, which of course I first used to buy a decent guitar.

On the field

Most of the time I lived in California I had a motorcycle and I loved going on rides, especially to the coast. Once I was actively playing in rock bands I didn't have as much time to ride, but I took advantage of it for the first few months. One ride took me to my first live baseball game. It was in the eighties in Oakland where I got to see my first Major League pitch. As the game was played and people ate their peanuts and popcorn, I discovered a lot of things an entrepreneur could learn from baseball.

On a baseball field the home plate, the pitcher, the catcher, and the crowd is life. I saw the role of the pitcher and catcher as your competition as they would work as a team to distract you, the batter. The catcher yells to the pitcher, "Throw him a slider." So you mentally and physically prepare for a slider, but within a split second, the blur of a curve ball you were completely unprepared for comes across the plate. You miss because you didn't see the secret hand signal, and the umpire yells, "Steeeerike!"

Do you call a do-over like we did in third grade? You could blame the catcher? If he wasn't telling jokes trying to cause you to lose focus you may have been able to hit the pitch. Do you complain to the umpire? You could blame the crowd. If they weren't so loud you would have been less distracted.

They have their own job to do and part of it is to distract you. Your job is to stay focused and block out or at least manage distractions so you can hit the ball. Do your job and quit worrying what others are doing because the goal is to win, and the one who does their job best wins.

People like to blame failures on anything but their own lack of focus and preparation. Every second you spend assigning blame is a second you could have been putting towards winning. How you play the game may be what builds character, but remember, winning is the goal. The score board doesn't care if the pitcher distracted you, it only cares what the numbers say after the game is over. Retired athletes traditionally do well because they learned how and why to focus on what will help them win as opposed to blame, which has become a plague in our society. Police, teachers, neighbors, senators, the President, the neighborhood code officer.... everyone's getting blamed for something.

The worst part of blame is how easy it can it become a habit. When people fail they instantly look for something or someone to blame it on without realizing they're at fault. Even if your blame is accurate and justified, it doesn't help you win.

In batting-school 101 you learned how to position your hands and how many inches to keep between your toes and the home plate. You even recall instruction on how to bend your knees and how to position your elbows. Those are the technical facets of the game. Now you have the mental side; things like blocking out distractions caused by the roar of the crowd and how to manage deception created between the pitcher and the catcher.

I hear people complain how their boss is a jerk, and they think the answer is to quit their job. At their next job the boss is great, but the pay stinks. They quit again, and the next job has a great boss, great pay, but they have to travel. It never ends.

Most excuses are easily justified. It wasn't your fault the company never sent their manager through a people-skills class so they could be a better leader to the staff. It wasn't your fault the company used profits for a jet instead of creating incentive programs for the employees. And it's not your fault many business owners are out of touch with happenings within the depths of their company. Unfortunately for the employee, the world often doesn't care how an employee is affected. However, this is often a benefit in disguise because someone "taking care of you" can develop into a form of personal dependency. Every employment position has advantages and disadvantages. As far as excuses go, you can make excuses, or you can make money. Pick one. I don't know anyone that makes both.

There's a story about two kids going on a job interview. They are asked how tall a local historical building is. The first kid is excited because he knows the answer, the question was on a recent test in school. Instantly he replies, "One hundred seven feet tall." The second kid was not in that particular class, but he has experience in HOW to think. He goes outside, compares his shadow to his height, then measures the building's shadow and begins to calculate. He returns to the job interview saying, "The building is a little over a hundred feet tall." The job is offered to the second kid, even though the first kid had the exact answer.

The first kid depended on memory, he would need guidance and an instruction manual to be productive. The second kid proved that he wasn't dependent on what he memorized from a class test and that he can figure things out. Which is worth more to a company? The lesson is how there's greater value in knowing HOW to think, as opposed to WHAT to think.

People believe if they won a million dollars they could quit working. I disagree. The reality is if most people were given a million dollars tomorrow, they'd never achieve the level of success of someone that earned their first million. If they knew how to manage money they wouldn't need to win it in the first place. Lack of money is not a problem. There's a whole sea of it out there. And financial challenges are not about having or not having money, they're about financial management skills. In most cases, if someone can't manage ten dollars properly they will not manage ten thousand any better. Lottery systems have studied how people win and end up broke a short time after. Never having earned money comes with never learning how to manage it.

That day in Oakland most of the crowd only got to enjoy a great ball game. I got a great ball game too, but I also got lessons that I was able to apply to so many facets of my life. While others were thinking about washing the drippings from their lunch off of their hands, I was thinking about what makes a winner. It was an excellent opportunity to learn from an experience.

Time to Rock-and-Roll!

Prior to moving from the Florida Keys to California I never touched a musical instrument. The only thing I played was the radio. To start the process moving forward I knew the best thing I could do was find local bands and start meeting musicians. It didn't take long to find them, and things began to happen.

At the time Google was little more than a couple guys at Stanford with an idea. Musicians found each other through bulletin boards at music stores where I once saw a "Bass player wanted" note with a phone number. I didn't play bass but I could keep up, and fellow musicians could always depend on me showing up for practice. I quickly discovered I had no musical talent. During my rock-and-roll days playing in various bands I got the opportunity to associate with some great talent, but when it came to my own I didn't have a drop. That was okay. Lucky for me, it wasn't about talent; it was about having big hair, looking cool, and tight leather clothing.

After an evening in one of the local night clubs my band went to the local pool hall. When that closed I often rode my motorcycle down bike trails along Sacramento's American River. It was about a hundred feet across in most places and listening to the flow at night helped me think. I'd find a log at the river's edge and sit there, sometimes till sunup. I ended up trading that motorcycle for three screws in my right ankle when it became part of the bumper of a Ford T-Bird on Folsom Boulevard that made a right turn in front of me. I spent three days in the hospital and was lucky to have survived.

Time passed and I took a job at a music store in downtown Sacramento, "Drum and Guitar City." It didn't pay as much as managing the car wash, but it got me closer to my dream, and it offered discounted prices on music gear to help support my new habit. Working there ended up being priceless. I got to associate with a lot of talent, plus the touring rock stars would occasionally stop in. This gave me an opportunity to meet and associate with the people I was dreaming to be.

The "Bammer," (AKA Bam Bam,) was a known bouncer at local clubs. The era reminded me of the fifties when it was the Greasers against the Jocks. Sacramento was a big college town, so we had short haired college students against the Rockers. A fight would almost always break out when the rockers showed up because once they did the college guys had little chance to "pick up" girls.

One night I got cornered by a group of jealous students and it was starting to look like blood was inevitable. (Blood was okay; just don't mess with the hair.) The Bammer came to my rescue. We didn't know each other well, but he recognized me from Sacramento's rock-and-roll night club scene. Here's where I discovered the value of who you associate with and who you're "connected" to. The college guys learned not to shove the Bammer. He broke up the tussle by throwing the guy with his finger in my face over a six-foot fence into the parking lot. Word got out that I fell under the protection of the Bammer, and I never got hassled again.

Local bands swapped members often, when you put that much ego and arrogance in a room together band members get caught up in quite a game of musical chairs. I was particular when it came to deciding who to play with. When a band broke up, which seemed to be weekly, I identified who brought the most talent to the table. To me it was business, so when it came time to pick sides, I didn't choose friends, I went where the talent was.

I played with many different bands and always associated my decisions with talent, something that has paid off in many ways, and a habit I still practice.

This was also the time of an arrest that woke me up. I was going from one party to another and cut a cop off as I pulled out of a convenience store. I jumped a curb and made my way through a chain onto a golf course to lose him, not realizing that by then there were several cops chasing me. (I forgot they had radios.) I got out of my truck wearing a leather trench coat that went down to my ankles and had hair past my waist. Had I exited any faster I most likely would have been gunned down by Sacramento's finest. I'm still grateful this one experience was the only wake-up call I needed. It was an expensive process, but nobody got hurt and I learned how to wash police cars in the winter in downtown Sacramento in the form of community service.

Selling possessions and packing up to move three thousand miles away to chase a fantasy of being a rock star was a bit crazy. I wasn't even an adult when all of this started. I looked and acted the part, but inside I was still a growing entrepreneur looking for my niche in the world. Inside, I was still the guy that would help an old lady cross the street, not that they would let me with my physical appearance at the time.

I had nobody to spend holidays with and nobody to buy gifts for, so while my band-mates would party on Christmas Eve I was downtown giving cartons of smokes to homeless people. Cigarettes may not have been thought of as the perfect gift, but it's what they wanted. What I wanted was for them to know that somebody was thinking about them. At the time I looked and acted the part, but that's all it was, an act. I was no rock star. Quitting rock-and-roll was a lot harder than I thought it would be, but I had to. I wanted so bad to fit in, but I had no talent.

Something told me that I didn't belong there, and I had been away from a place I could call home for long enough. It was time to move on.

Almost everyone I knew in the music scene had some kind of addiction. Something chained all of us to the lifestyle. The addictions weren't always threatening, but they were addictions by definition. Mine wasn't sex, drugs or alcohol. My addiction was a need for attention.

I often thought about the Bon Jovi video that started it all, but that wasn't the beginning. What my childhood lacked created the need I had for attention. That's what started it all, and that's what triggered the pursuit of rock-and-roll. Without realizing it, what I saw years prior was the attention the band was getting.

I woke up from my rock-and-roll coma and realized it was time to make some decisions. I don't remember much from the few math classes I attended, but I understood the philosophy of how the quickest way from A to B was a straight line. So I quit rock-and-roll the quickest way I could think of; I shaved my head. No hair meant no rock band. Including no job at a music store either.

Plotting a new course
Leaving the world of rock-and-roll had me feeling like I was tossed out of a tornado. The past few years were like a dream. Memories were blurry... but I was told I had a great time. I had no idea who I was or what I was going to do. Soon enough, shock wore off and it was time to consider a new course. I took a job as a dishwasher in a country club because it included food. I worked an afternoon to midnight shift, but I went in early and worked a couple hours for free so I could get lunch. I worked with a chef that just returned from a culinary school in Paris who taught me the art of cooking, plus the owner of the club was a dentist so I was also able to have dental work updated for free.

I was emotionally lost but not for long. I shook it off, leaned into the wind, and the anticipation of my next adventure soon had me on the edge of my seat.

It was all over in my early twenties and I was so excited to have lived that life. It was time to make money and move on. I was motivated by watching peers get sucked in to what happens to guys in bands

that don't have a lot of talent. Most couldn't quit.
They each had different addictions, and just couldn't
shake it. I saw where most of them ended up and I
didn't want to be there. Managing a band or working
in promotions was closer to my talents, but that
didn't interest me.

There's a big difference between goals and dreams.
For me, a goal is clearly defined, written down, and
has a date on it. I never had a goal of being Jon Bon
Jovi. It was a dream and maybe a fantasy, but never a
goal. I lived the dream, and I treasure the memory,
but I was also strong enough to know it was time to
turn the page and start a new chapter.

Earlier in life people had sympathy for me as a
runaway, but since they didn't live it, they didn't
understand its advantages. One is that I didn't know
boundaries. Not knowing where the "line" was made
me push things further which develops a character
not willing to settle for mediocrity. Another was that
I did everything alone. Alone means no misdirection
from people trying to protect me. Alone has
disadvantages, but I wasn't alone for long, and I
learned why to listen to some, and not to others.

We all make decisions that steer our life, and we all
have friends that want to chip in on those decisions.
They mean no harm, but the closer you are
emotionally to someone, the less likely they would

advise you to take chances or do anything that may involve risk. Sometimes they're saving you, but sometimes they're preventing you from being successful. So many people warned me not move to California in pursuit of being the next Bon Jovi. (Perhaps because he lived in New Jersey.) I would have missed out of this entire experience had I listened to others, not to mention how my life would have been missing a chapter I would have never even know about. It makes one wonder what could be remembered if you're willing to pursue dreams.

Our friends and peers will often encourage us to take routes of little or no risk. If they advise to play it safe and you do, you'll never know what could have been. No harm done and they're safe. If they suggest you do not step out of the box, and against their advice you do and crash, they're still safe. On the flip-side, if they advise you to take a chance and things don't work out, they could be to blame and the friendship may be on the line. Any way you make the split, they're secure if they advise you to play it safe and not take chances.

People offer different advice to a stranger than they would a friend. With a stranger, there's no personal risk involved.

The key to taking advice is not always the advice itself, sometimes it's about qualifying who to take it from. Are they qualified to give you that particular advice? Is your advisor speaking of theory or have they lived it? People only know what they've experienced and what they have been exposed to. Unless your friends are going to cover your bills and responsibilities, do your own homework and make your own decisions.

I see this a lot when someone gets involved with a multi-level marketing business. People develop a vision that turns to a dream of getting out of a nine-to-five life. While most of these businesses are legal, moral, and great opportunities, our friends have most likely heard of someone else's nightmare story, and they think they're doing you a favor by trying to talk you out of it. What they're usually saying, without realizing it is: "If you chase your dreams and catch them, I'll look bad because I'm afraid to chase mine." Or perhaps, "I'm afraid of rejection, I don't have a lot of confidence in myself, and I'm worried my friends will laugh at me, or I'd join you."

It's important not to think less of your friends if they offer safe advice that holds you back. They don't know any better. As we merge into a world of friends being a link we click on as opposed to someone we can talk to and trust, people are losing the knowledge of how to be a friend. If they knew what advice to offer, or how to, they would.

JIM GRIFFITHS

CHAPTER FIVE

GOING DUTCH

My room-mate in Sacramento, Keith, was quite a friend. At the time he was working two jobs while attending Sacramento State College full time. Keith had little time for a friendship, but we spent a lot of late nights talking ourselves to sleep. I continued washing dishes at the country club in Sacramento till I figured out where I would land next. This was a meaningless thing to be doing, which I saw a lot of value in. Meaningless time offers great thinking time, if you use it for that.

By some, idle time is considered Satan's work. I see it as a necessity if you want to think creatively. Few people can solve complex problems while busy and stressed out or under pressure.

I heard about people making a lot of money quick in Alaska's commercial fishing industry. I flipped through the local paper's classified section and saw an ad that said, "Make $30,000 in three months fishing in Alaska." It included a toll-free number with a recording asking you to send in a hundred dollars for the program, which was a book that included everything you needed to know about getting a job and who to contact. After a couple trips to Seattle for interviews, I left Sacramento and puddle-jumped my way to Dutch Harbor, Alaska.

Alaska's fishery turned out to be the perfect place to make money for a broke musician trying to work his way back to Florida. There was a lot of down-time for thinking. At first I was disappointed I didn't become a rock star, but after a long cold winter fishing in Alaska I realized it was not meant to be. It's not where my talents were, and I remain grateful to have discovered this at a young age.

While working in Alaska I learned about sleep deprivation, how to be less attractive to a bear, and the importance of keeping my feet and hands warm. I got to see the Alaska tourists don't get the opportunity to experience, and I flew with some interesting bushmen. At one time my duffel bag had thirty-six tags on it from jumping island-to-island on small planes. I watched a bear pull in a land-based fishing net for an easy lunch, I made a lot of money, and I had a priceless opportunity so few would understand the benefit of in our noisy digital world of texting, social media and the ongoing distractions which seem to consume our days.

Alaska offered valuable "think time" which allows the ability to check your compass. It makes me wonder how many are suffering from a lack of direction with all the multitasking people do today.

The company I went to work for was based in Seattle and owned several fishing oriented operations in Alaska. I could go home for a few weeks in between fishing seasons, or have them send me from one job to another. Between sea and land based fisheries there was always something to do. One job was on a four-hundred foot ship that was a floating processor with an onboard cannery. We'd cut through ice to reach the fishing grounds then drag nets for six weeks, off-load to a freighter at sea, then fish for six more weeks. I worked eighteen-hour shifts and it was very physical.

Between seasons I got a temporary land-based job in a town called Naknek. The job was at a cannery and I was a cook, which offered much better working conditions than fishing jobs. I spent down-time sitting on a beach in thought. A "beach" for us was a strip of rocks where if you dug about a foot down you'd hit ice. I worked hard and held my own under extreme conditions and I was accepted by my co-workers. I had moved up in rank fast and had a promising future in the industry if I wanted it. Most guys worked hard for six months and sat on a real beach in Mexico for six. What a life!

I was in my early twenties and it was decision time. I sat on that shoreline and contemplated if I should stay and pursue a career in Alaska, or take my chances in what we called the "Lower 48." The work was hard but the money was good, and I was in the best physical shape of my life. We could tell the truth without the worry of being politically correct. The small towns had almost no crime and no therapist available to help overcome emotional scars if someone offended you. If a storm came through, people could die, so risks from weather to wild animals created an environment where we could count on each other. If we stepped on someone's toes, we worked it out without taking them to court.

I had people skills for where I was, but the kind of people skills I had may work against me if I were to return to the states. I was a round peg in a round hole in Alaska, but I'd have to adjust that social style if I wanted to pass the "Terminal Test" in the states.

The Terminal Test

I watched a video of people in an office lobby waiting their turn at a job interview. They slouched, slept, checked their social media, and did just about anything else you could imagine outside of preparing for their interview. What they didn't know was the decision makers were watching their behavior on camera, which would partially determine who stayed and who may be invited to join the company.

I encourage education, but no college degree can match the ability to interact with other people when it comes to making things happen. We're forced to drive the speed limit and learn math, but our society has no requirement to do the one thing that every successful person claims to be the most important factor; interaction with others. Talking, listening, reading body language and basic communication skills are slowly fading from society. People who can maintain the ability to pass the Terminal Test will have a great advantage over any other form of education. Here it is:

This has most likely been demonstrated a few ways, mine takes place in a train station. A storm has shut down the tracks and the place is packed. You're sitting next to the same person for seven hours. There's no WiFi signal and no cell phone service. (It's like you're stuck in the seventies.)

Two weeks later the person you were sitting next to is at a family barbeque and Uncle Bob asks how the trip to Denver was. How do they describe the person, (you,) they spent seven hours sitting next to at the train station during miserable conditions? Did they even remember you? Were you boring? Did you talk at all? Did you not shut up the whole time? Did you spent seven hours complaining about the delay? Did they rave about how they met the most unique person on their trip and how the delay was actually a memorable experience? Would someone remember you at all? Were you so fascinating that they wanted your contact information to keep in touch? Did they enjoy your company, or did they ignore you and pretend they were sleeping?

Our digital world has been credited for connecting people, but at the same time it has drastically disconnected us. While we may be connected digitally, we're not emotionally. Social media companies were faced with a challenge most never knew or would have understood; how to bridge the gap between emotional creatures, (people,) and computers.

This is why some made it big while others we hardly even remember. People make emotional decisions creating a gap between computers and people. Words such as "Like" and "Friend" are known tools to bridge this gap. When 827 people "Like" a video we posted, we feel good. When we have 1,293 "Friends," we feel good. "Feel" is the key word here.

A few inches over the top of your phone you'll find a whole world full of people, and one day you're going to have to talk to, relate to, and earn respect from some of them. Society is losing valuable social skills as technology attaches us to four inch screens of glass, and if people were to trace their history of things that didn't work out, more often than not it leads back to someone not relating to you personally.

A lot of marriage counselors have a secret weapon on a shelf in their office. It's a book called "The Five Love Languages." It's about how we as people don't speak the same language. It's not a reference to Spanish or English, it's about how we can say something, yet the person we're talking to hears something else. We say and describe things as we see them, and if the person you're talking to doesn't speak the same language, they hear something different. This is a golden magic pill for couples having communication difficulty.

First understand different languages exist, then observe the other person to see what language they'd understand. Your goal is to identify their language and learn how to say things in a way the other person would understand what you meant to communicate. Also, if a person has a soft character and you naturally speak with an aggressive tone, they may not hear what you're saying. You may see solutions in your head, while they need it explained in words. You want to be the one who adjusts to their language, don't expect the opposite.

Pay attention to the other person's pupils. If they're fluctuating and flickering, their brain is working harder to understand what you're saying. This is not for couples only. Managers, neighbors, business owners and coworkers would all experience impressive results if this one basic skill was practiced.

You've heard how priceless word-of-mouth is, how do people feel and what are they saying about you? It's "Marketing 101." People think marketing is for business, while we socially market ourselves every day. Quality people will not likely befriend you if they don't relate to you. And if people don't relate to you, they don't trust you. And if they don't trust you, they're less likely to do business with you. It's not about scoring high or passing the test every time, it's about having the skills and ability to pass.

Go sit on a park bench somewhere and practice passing the Terminal Test.

Burning excuses

On that shoreline in Alaska, while wondering if I could ever pass the Terminal Test if I were to return to the "Lower 48," I made a list of reasons I would have not likely been a success in a different environment; no friends, little work experience, a lack of confidence, no high school diploma, I got kicked out of the Coast Guard, I had a poor relationship with my parents, I didn't get along with others well, etc. This was on paper and I kept writing. It turned out to be a list of excuses as to why I wouldn't be a success anywhere. I was about to make a life-altering decision for the wrong reasons. I read the excuse list a few times and burned it. I left what I thought was holding me back, which was all in my head, on a rocky shoal in Alaska.

On my desk today is a jar of rocks I collected from that shoreline. It's a visual reminder to not let imaginary problems stop me from doing anything.

Not only physically, but I had also mentally burned my excuses. I decided to leave Alaska and return to the lower states to start some kind of business. I also decided that if anything would stop me from being a success, it would not be a list of excuses on a piece of paper.

JIM GRIFFITHS

CHAPTER SIX

THE VALUE OF MENTORS

A few seasons working in Alaska put me in a very lonely spot but at the same time it helped the process of gathering thoughts. I was away for months and lost touch with band members, I had no career path, and I was three thousand miles from the only place I thought I could call home. I was ready to work my way back to Florida. A quick stop in Sacramento to say goodbye and tie up a few loose ends was all I had left to do.

I felt a need to visit an old friend before I left America's west coast. Jay was much older than I, he was wealthy, and though our lifestyles had little in common we were both driven and understood the concept of being different. I'm not quite sure how I've managed to attracted mentors like this, but I believe there to be an unwritten law in society about how certain characters are naturally attracted to others. Our conversations were often like a mathematician telling a four-year-old kid about an advanced trigonometric formula able to bond two structures. In my case, he was trying to advise me on success principles I didn't understand, yet would one day make sense and benefit my life.

Jay was the first person I spent time with who was naturally gifted when it came to the art of communicating with others. He expressed on many occasions how he felt human communication was fading from society, and the importance of efforts to prevent it. He saw the ability to effectively communicate with others to be a priority and he always managed to find a way to communicate where I could comprehend what he was trying to tell me. Jay was always planting seeds and knew one day it would all make sense. In way we hardly knew each other, but he knew people and why they do things they do, and I was grateful he was willing to pass on what he could. He also had a way of knowing what I was ready for, and what I wasn't.

There's an old joke about a preacher showing up on a Sunday morning and only one person is in the audience. He decides if it's one or one hundred people, he's here to deliver his best. That morning out comes his longest and most powerful sermon ever and the one person who showed up says, "I'm a farmer, and if only one cow showed up for dinner I'd put out the feed, but I wouldn't dump the whole load on her!"

I've got quite a history of mentors. I see them as people who help me believe in myself and lead me to the "next step" so to speak. Some have been business and some are personal, some mixed it all together. Jay was one of the many mentors that I learned from, and like a good mentor, he never gave me more than I could handle. He was more like a personal coach by how he would ask penetrating questions to identify what I needed, then push me to the edge, but not over it.

I've always been one to take on the world all at once but Jay helped me understand how focusing on one step at a time helps solidify a task before moving to the next. The opposite would be doing fifteen things at once, what we today refer to as "multitasking," where things hardly ever get done efficiently.

Another long talk we had was about how we as people can't take on the world till we take on ourselves, as in facing our own fears, demons and personal challenges. Today I see younger people have a desire to fight for a cause worthy of a good fight, yet they never learned how to identify and tackle their own troubles. How can you go out and save the world if you haven't first saved yourself?

Sometimes I think people get buried in the world's problems as a way of running from their own.

Years ago the skills needed to be a responsible adult were acquired from the family unit in the home. As the concept of the "American Home" dissolves in our society I see no source for younger people to learn how to create their own personal foundation. Some cultures require you to prove you're ready to be an adult, but in our nation adulthood only requires being alive 6,570 days. As the needed skills to operate as an adult fade each generation will suffer more. Mentors can help fill this gap.

When Jay and I befriended each other I was in my early twenties and not a big reader, which was something he was on my case about. I now read a lot and find books to be breadcrumb trails left behind by people who overcame challenges and went on to do things I want to do. I wish more people would make time to incorporate priceless information in the form of printed words into their lives.

Jay recommended a specific book promising it would be a quick read. He claimed it would eventually help me find my niche in the world. Instructions were to find a quiet place and sit under a tree, somewhere peaceful with no distractions. The book was Jonathan Livingston Seagull by Richard Bach. I drove through the Sahara Mountains from Sacramento to Lake Tahoe where I sat under a tree and opened the book. It took less than an hour to read, and it was a game changer.

The story offers various meanings depending on where you are in life. For me it was about knowing you have what it takes to do more. Jonathan was a seagull that didn't want scraps of food from fishing boats. He wasn't comfortable with handouts and he didn't want to just "get by" with the flock. He wanted to fly and discover. To this day, the story reminds me of accomplishment. I've always had a habit of trying harder when people around me claimed something couldn't be done. Sometimes, as the title of this book goes, the reason I did something was because I was told I couldn't do it. Many things I've applied myself to confused others because it didn't need to be done, but doing them anyway created a habit that led to figuring out how to make things happen.

Jay and I had a lot of long talks, and he knew my childhood planted a lot of insecurities in my character. He also knew I played in rock-bands because they accepted me. We all have a craving to be accepted.

An entrepreneur wants to be accepted too. They're often looked at as an outcast for separating themselves from the herd and doing things differently. But when they accomplish and succeed, they're looked at as eccentric. That gap in between, when you're not accepted, can easily and dangerously take control of your compass.

Jay was trying to teach me about acceptance, and what you're willing to trade for it. The craving for acceptance is normal, but if you do things for the purpose of being accepted you put yourself at risk of getting a reverse effect. A need for acceptance may point towards a lack of self-respect. What you may subconsciously be looking for is respect from other people to take the place of respect you may not have for yourself. Focus on goals and do things for the sense of accomplishment. This leads to a true sense of personal acceptance, which creates the double-edged sword of respect. These are things a mentor can help you maintain and understand.

Since I didn't get a lot of acceptance as a kid I craved it later in life. This is what drove me to playing in rock bands. It also made pursuing a life of entrepreneurism difficult because of that gap between outcast and eccentric. I refer to that gap as "the tube," and how everyone has their own tube(s) to go through. Most are emotional while some may be physical. If you make it through your tubes, you deserve and get to keep what's on the other side. If you feel like you're in your "tube" now you're probably doing things right.

Jay and I once talked about the difference between having people respect you as opposed to whether or not they like you. I always figured those two as the same thing. A few months ago I was having breakfast at a political action committee meeting where our local Sheriff was invited to be the guest presenter of the day. He has a reputation of being a dynamic speaker and he's been a great contributor to our community. Our Sheriff had just announced running for reelection and the community was excited to get brought up to speed on his office and to hear his plans for the next four years.

This particular Sheriff had been in the position for several terms and when there was an election he was known to win an overwhelming percentage of the community's support. He was respected nationwide and had a reputation of doing his job well. In the past I've volunteered with his department and heard comments from active officers. They respect him as much as the public does, and it all points to character.

He's good with people, tough on crime, and he's held media accountable on many occasions. Our Sheriff is known to do the right thing even if there's personal consequences involved. He's maintained strong support during his entire career, and the position of heading the Sheriff's Office had little chances of being available till he decided to voluntarily pass it on.

A guy sitting next to me at the breakfast commented on how everyone just loved this Sheriff. Bla Bla Bla!

He went on and on to a point of me almost getting annoyed because it was distracting. His comments led me to believe he did not approve of this Sheriff, and it all pointed to an incident about a year prior. I recalled the incident. It was a case of "fake-news" as opposed to what really happened. It would have been nice if this guy knew the facts before breathing his lack of knowledge all over me.

My attempt to stop him from distracting me was by explaining how the Sheriff holds an elected position and he could soon exercise his constitutional right to vote for someone else. He said, "No, I'm voting for this guy, I just don't like him."

Mentors are someone you learn from and can be more than a friend you physically talk with. Though I didn't socialize with the Sheriff personally I considered him to be a mentor through his actions and reputation. Many times when faced with a tough decision I would wonder, "What would the Sheriff do?" This could be considered a form of "silent" or "absent" mentorship.

We all want people to like us. That's why social websites use the word "like" as an icon to click on. Social media developers knew this would create an emotional substitute for human interaction. There's a lot of people I like but don't necessarily respect. And there are also a lot of people I respect even if I don't like them. Acquiring both is great, but if you must choose, choose respect.

I liked, trusted, and respected my friend and mentor Jay, and I knew he had a good reason for asking me to learn about acceptance. I think he knew I was insecure from experiences in my childhood. I would imagine he picked up on me looking for acceptance from him and wanted to help me understand that I didn't need it. Another topic of conversation we had was about what motivates people to do what we do. Most do things out of habit or because it's what they've always done. They're comfortable doing it. We talked about how you should do something because of the results you get, not because you like to do it.

Jay also tried to help me discover what I was passionate about. He went to college to study chemistry and made his fortune in real estate. He had no passion for chemistry, but he loved closing a deal on a piece of property, so he pursued something he was able to put passion into.

I was once asked to do a talk about why we as people do what we do for a group of college students. I started with a philosophy of hanging wallpaper. It was a younger crowd so I had to first explain what wallpaper was and how it was installed, then asked who wanted to join me. No hands went up. I added how it paid ten-grand a week, you only had to work three hours a day, and after two years you got a full pension for life. I again asked who wanted to join me and every hand went up. I explained how why you do something will always overpower what you're doing.

This was years ago and I now have mixed feelings about the wallpaper philosophy. If you're not able to put passion into what you do, results suffer. And if you don't produce quality results, you may find yourself going around in circles wondering why things are not working the way you want them to.

It's important to have mentors in your life. Even people like Bill Gates talk about associating with people that inspire him and offer ideas he may not have considered. He's "connected," something my friend Jay helped me understand the value of. And I found this to be as true in a rock-and-roll band as it would be in a board room. In rock-and-roll I was friends with a club owner which gave my band more opportunities to be on the club's calendar, I was friends with Bam-Bam the bouncer which kept me from getting beat up by college students, and I made friends with the manager of a furniture storage company that turned into a place for my band to practice at night. Ultimately, being "connected" is what caused my bands to get out where we could be seen and discovered by a scout.

Both the car wash and music store I worked at in Sacramento while pretending to be a rock star in the eighties offered an honest wage, but I felt like I could do more. Having mentors such as Jay and others like him helped me understand my own potential and made it easy to leave Sacramento to go out into the world in search of what could be next.

JIM GRIFFITHS

CHAPTER SEVEN

THE ALASKA QUEST

The saying, "In the groove," is known to be a sailing term about positioning a vessel just right. It's a combination of adjusting sails and balancing weight properly to achieve maximum efficiency while underway.

Being gone for so long had me feeling "Out of the groove," so I said goodbye to California and returned to Florida. I was in my mid-twenties and excited to get right to work. After what I had just experienced commercial fishing in Alaska, a job now would seem like a vacation.

Soon after I returned, I lost my only sister. She developed breast cancer at age twenty-eight and died at age thirty-eight. Here I was after such a positive life changing experience facing my first family death. I didn't handle it very well, but my childhood helped me develop the ability to bury my feelings. So that's what I did, and I went to work.

I had a little money in the bank from commercial fishing, but a little money in the bank is no money in the bank if you spend it. I needed cash flow. Since I knew the business, I took a job at a car wash till I crossed paths with my next adventure.

I was living in a hotel for $95 a week with a take-home pay of about $120. I depended on tips if I wanted more than peanut butter & jelly sandwiches. I knew this wouldn't last long, and it was actually refreshing. Struggling with limited resources is good practice for when life throws an unexpected economic curve ball.

Even at minimum wage jobs my work ethics have always gone far beyond an employer's expectations. Not for them, but for me. It was my character that would suffer if I didn't prove to be an efficient and productive worker. I see many people with jobs get hung up on work ethics. They have no desire to go the "extra mile" because they feel the company doesn't appreciate or deserve the commitment.

Don't do it for them, do it for you. If you're lazy and become a clock-milker for any reason, you pay for it more than the company. They'll replace you with the worst case scenario being another clock-milker. You, on the other hand, are the one who loses by not developing a how-to-win character.

If you develop a rock star attitude on the job, yes the company benefits and may not appreciate you, but you're also developing a quality working character in demand by another company willing pay you what you're worth. You'll never be on that company's radar if you've got bad work habits. There's a time to be selfish, so forget about the company and worry about your own personal work habits and ethics.

My willingness to work harder than expected as a minimum wage laborer at a car wash got me bumped to the detail shop which included a pay increase and more tips, so now I could move into a studio apartment. It was small but much larger than the hotel I'd been living at, it was clean, and it became the birthplace of my next adventure.

The "Alaska Quest" was a book set I sold through the mail. I got the idea for this business when I recalled how I got the commercial fishing job in Alaska, which was a reply to a classified ad in a newspaper. (That's how us old-timers did things before the web.) The package I received by answering the classified ad was a book that had information about the working environment and what to expect in Alaska, depending what time of year you were there. It included job types and descriptions, plus contacts to over a hundred companies that hired people to work in the various industries.

I couldn't get this out of my head; I spent over a hundred dollars for a few pages of information that was photo copied for pennies. I saw money in this, so the entrepreneur light started to glow, and I went to work.

I rewrote the information in my own words and included contacts to the companies in Seattle that handled human resources. Personal computers, graphic software, and even internet access was limited at the time, but I was able to buy what was known as a desktop publishing machine. This device was bulky and had a small square black-and-white screen that showed an idea where your art or text would end up, but the only way to know what a page was going to look like was to print one and have a look. Once I got pages laid out, I hired an office supply store to make copies, I folded them in half making a booklet, and there, I was a publisher. Now how do I promote and sell them?

Mail order was booming at the time and it was hard to watch TV without seeing an infomercial soliciting a book called "Newspapers, Newspapers, Newspapers". It was a directory of newspapers all over the country. With this tool I would have the ability to place classified ads all over the US to sell The Alaska Quest, my pirated three-book set about how to get a job in Alaska.

I placed classified ads in newspapers around the country that lead to a toll-free number with a recording similar to the one that talked me into buying the hundred-dollar book, but mine was different. Mine had three books with three different sets of information, and mine was only $39.95 for the whole set. "And if you act now, we'll throw in a list of companies that hire regularly."

I never talked to a person. My phone bill enabled me to know how many people called my toll-free number, and I could compare that to how many people ordered the book set. At first it was about twenty calls a week with zero sales. I then modified the recording till I got a sale, and just kept changing the recording till the ratio increased.

Sales or no sales usually points to marketing, something I knew nothing about, so my averages were not so good at first. Street smarts told me people took action based on how they felt emotionally, so I focused on a way to stimulate a potential buyer's senses in my promotions. This makes a lot of today's advertising agencies almost useless. People today think marketing is about how many people click on a website or "Like" a social media page. It's not. Results are what you're looking for, and numbers could never match emotional stimulation when it comes to results.

Marketing is, and always will be, the act of creating something that triggers an emotional response strong enough to cause your potential customer to take action. People that sell advertising know how to "sell," not market. Those are two different things. If they knew marketing they'd be marketing themselves better and wouldn't have to sell so much.

In my eyes, the most important task on my desk was to have the classified advertisements and phone recording worded in a way that would trigger an emotional response. At first I thought placing expensive ads in known cities would produce. It didn't. The trick was to go with small towns. Those people had less local opportunity and were more willing to travel for seasonal work that paid big money. The classified ads I placed in known towns were priced from thirty to fifty dollars and ran for a week. The newspaper ads that ran in small towns were only five to ten dollars a week. So I spent less and got more.

Constantly shifting gears and trying different techniques, some that made little sense, ended up offering positive results. One week over thirty checks arrived and I thought I was on my way to big business. The problem now was cashing the checks. I didn't have a business checking account. I didn't even have a business. I was still living in a studio apartment and was running a mail order business!

I discontinued pursuit of the Alaska Quest. Most people would wonder why I would bother if I had no plans to turn it into something more. It had potential, but it didn't excite me. If I'm not excited, I make it work to prove to myself I can, then I move on. To me, something like this is a confidence builder, a way of sharpening my sword, and practice for when you cross paths with more worthy projects.

Some would look at the Alaska Quest book set as a failed business because it didn't profit long-term. I was practicing being an entrepreneur, and I've since applied what I learned to other business ventures. I also learned how valuable information was. From knowing how to evade dinosaurs to what the next hot stock is going to be, information has always been almost as valuable as life itself. Understanding the value of information caused my next business to dominate its own industry.

Most people trade time for dollars with a lack of understanding how to make something pay off residually. From my perspective, I'm still making money off the Alaska Quest today, and will for the rest of my life.

JIM GRIFFITHS

CHAPTER EIGHT

THE WAXMAN

What started as a way to make extra money on my days off turned out to be a strong business that supported me well for years.

Working in the detail shop earned decent money, but the answer to "How much is enough?" is "A little bit more." So on my days off I walked through my neighborhood knocking on doors trying to wash cars for ten dollars. At the time, washing four cars meant collecting forty dollars, and forty dollars bought a bag of food for the week.

One day while working at the car wash the owner of a construction clean-up company asked if we could clean his trucks on Sundays. It was the only day his trucks were not being used and he wanted them to always look clean and presentable. The shop could not accommodate him, but I was off on Sundays, so I asked where the trucks were left on Saturday evenings and if he'd consider having me come to his shop to do the job. Once a week I washed his trucks, wiped the dash, and under the seat was an envelope with twenty dollars per truck.

There were always five or six trucks parked at his office, so I made at least a hundred bucks in one day. It was a nice chunk of change for someone working at a car wash, and worth a lot more money than washing cars in my neighborhood, though I did all three. Other people got a job at that car wash around the same time I did. Months later they had the same job and the same personal income as when they started. Their "get by" attitude prevented them from advancing.

Within a few months I went from a car wash job to working in the detail shop, I washed cars in my neighborhood on days off, and I had a Sunday gig for an additional hundred bucks a week. My income was around triple compared to people I worked with, and I didn't do one thing that anyone else couldn't have done. I believe in luck, but I believe more about how what we get is a reflection of what we're willing to put out.

I saw there could be money in the vehicle cleaning business so instead of the stereo or motorcycle I wanted, I invested in towels, various detailing supplies, a bottle of wax, and I knocked on doors again. This time I offered to wash and wax cars for forty dollars. A few months later I owned a new pickup truck with "Waxman" in vinyl lettering across the windshield. I was waxing motor homes, cars, boats, and even small planes. Business exploded and I had so many return calls that there was no room for new business. I was a one-man-show and locally branded as the Waxman. I had no competition till a few years later when I was ready to sell the business anyway.

This went on for a few years and I loved every facet of the business. I owned a company in America, I was good at it, and I had an identity. I was the WAXMAN! It was a great business but working in the sun and running electric buffers took a toll on my body. It was time to consider shifting gears.

What created my next career was right under my nose for years, and something I looked at every day, but never thought of it as a business opportunity. (I wonder how many of those are in front of us regularly.)

My next adventure developed from advice offered by a mentor. We talked about how my shoulder was getting tired from the daily grind of the wax business and I wanted to build a different company that was less physical. He suggested I imagine hovering over our community and think about what people residing in it could use. I was advised not to get hung up on skills. There's skills, talents, and gifts. Gifts are unique, talents can be mastered with practice, but skills are something you can teach yourself.

At the time I lived in a coastal community with over six hundred miles of canal waterways and about forty water-access restaurants. I doubt anyone moved there to go hiking. It was all about the coastal environment, and there had to be something the coastal community needed.

My next adventure was disguised as a piece of paper I kept in the glove box of the Waxmobile. It was a list of businesses associated to the local marine community. I would photocopy a few sheets at a time and keep them handy as referrals for clients I waxed boats for. It was something I did as a service for customers, and the marine businesses loved having their name passed around. I had dedicated customers with or without doing things like this for them, but I saw it as a way of offering more value to my clients. Doing the minimum required and not continually offering more value to those who put food on your table is why many people will wake up in the same place year after year economically.

This is an example of how going over and beyond has unseen rewards. Without realizing it at the time, I was forming relationships with local marine businesses, and that was about to pay off. One day I got a call from a business that wasn't on the list asking what I would charge to put him on it. My tired body and worn shoulders were about to have some pressure taken off of them.

That list of local businesses on a sheet of paper turned into a monthly magazine I spent a year building the foundation for, and the Waxman was no longer.

I wanted to tell this story because opportunities are all around us. I found a need in society and turned it into a service. I looked around and got ideas from existing enterprises, and capitalized on every resource I could find. I found better ways to do things, and I worked hard.

People commented about how much business I had as the Waxman and how lucky I was to have so many clients. They only saw the results. Where were they when I was walking the neighborhood trying to make ten dollars with a bucket of soap? You've got to be willing to struggle through the early stages.

The foundation to a lot of business empires only took a year. It may have taken twenty years to find or develop an idea, or to act on something, but in most cases when someone had a plan and made a decision to dig in and commit, it only took a year to get the base established.

Many people get a couple months into a commitment and complain about time off and how you need balance in life. The thought of maintaining a balanced life is often used as justification to avoid doing things. Stuff that balance in a sock, bury your head in the sand, and build a foundation you'll be able to live on for the rest of your life. Softball, fishing and horseshoes will be there when you're ready.

The most common mistake I see people make when starting a new project is thinking they've already put in a lot of ground-work because of past experiences. Most haven't. Experience can bring knowledge to help make more informed decisions, and you may have contacts, but you've still got to start over as far as building a foundation for a company.

When you start a new project, you start a new timer. Having experience and contacts will help, but it doesn't necessarily shave anything off the clock.

Rewards go to those willing to push through that first year of learning, mistakes, and the endurance it takes to build a foundation. That first year is when doubt sets in, it's when friends warn you of possible failures, and it's what tests your endurance. It's what separates achievers from those that wake up in the same place thirty years from now.

The Waxman business served me well. It was great money and I learned a lot about building customer relationships. Its future needed to be someone else's dream, so after my next company was established and secure, I sold the Waxman for the cost of inventory and supplies.

JIM GRIFFITHS

CHAPTER NINE

NAUTICAL MILE

" **N**autical Mile" is a source of information for a popular coastal community in Florida in the form of a printed magazine. This company has an interesting story because of my zero experience in the industry, and how that's what actually made it work. This project started as a free one-page brochure I never planned to take further, and within a couple years became the most successful business of its kind in the state of Florida.

The Birth
Everything we do has some kind of motivational factor behind it, and the power of that motivation may be what determines how far you go. Sometimes it's financial, while other times it may be fear. My drive this time was curiosity. I couldn't help but wonder why an information source did not exist in a coastal community with miles of beaches, thirty-two boat ramps, thirty-six water-access restaurants,

fourteen bait shops and forty in-water marinas. Thousands of people move to this area annually and there was no information source to explore its coastal community. It's not like people moved there to go hiking! I just had to find out why.

One thing had me hung up; why hasn't someone else already done it? The second layer to my curiosity was if I stumbled across something others hadn't thought of, perhaps it would turn into a great business. And that's exactly what happened.

As it turned out, there were a few similar informational sources in the area, I just didn't know they existed till I started looking for them.

Discovering the competition was when I got excited because I found them to offer little value to their readership or the community. Their focus was to sell advertising. They'd mix a bit of information between the pages to satisfy the perception of value, but it wasn't enough to stimulate people into becoming a "fan" of their product.

Beware of the perception of value. Magicians do not make an elephant disappear in the middle of a shopping mall. This is done by creating the perception of making an elephant disappear. People know it was a trick, and leaving them in suspense wondering how it was done keeps them coming back for more. The magician who wants continued success must help people develop the desire to see another trick. The opposite results occur when a business tricks customers with the perception of value.

I knew something specific would make Nautical Mile the best. When creating a business from scratch, I look for that one magical secret everything else circles around, and I consider it to be my job. A person creating an enterprise can be very productive when they find out what their job is. Mine was to make coastal enthusiasts want to be a fan of my product. If I could do that, I knew everything else would fall into place.

I wanted Nautical Mile's brand to be value as opposed to just another "fishing rag" that sold advertising space. I couldn't help but wonder what would happen if I put sales on hold, continued working the mobile wax business as a way to pay the initial overhead, and focus on piling up as much information as I could. As potential advertisers saw how many people picked up my product because it offered more information, they would see it as a better investment of their promotional dollars. My vision included advertisers dropping competitors and lining up to join me, which I was told couldn't be done. (Again, those magic words!) After being advised by peers in the industry this would be a disaster, my way led to being the last one standing.

I didn't put anyone out of business, they did it on their own by selling something that offered no value. Competitors were more focused on selling than providing information to the community. It was as if they had no respect for who put food on the table in their home.

I never started a business because I had an idea. I started one because I found a way to make it work.

I do that by breaking an idea up into facets to get a better understanding of what it will involve, then decide if I think it's worth pursuing. In private business classes I teach a process opposite of thinking out-of-the-box. The saying has become passive to a point of thinking but not acting, so I recreated it.

In a classroom I put a small cardboard box on the floor and ask people to list everything involved in the project we're discussing. Staff, software, building a website, if it would benefit by having a social media presence and who would manage it, how long before it would profit, insurance, marketing strategy, an exit plan, short and long term investments, etc.

I don't stop till there's twenty or thirty things listed. All of that goes INTO the box, and we look at it for ten seconds. I look around the room and ask, "Are you sure you want to pursue this?" After understanding exactly what this project would involve, including how long it would take to profit, risks, growth potential, and how much time and effort would need to be invested, sometimes the answer is no.

If the answer is yes, I place the box across the room and as a group we start making a list of what needs to be done in order to get what's in that box. It's a way of creating a business plan and an action plan all in one, with a better understanding of exactly what we need to do. So many people buy an occupational license and a box of business cards without dedicating a minute to developing a plan of action and wonder why it didn't work.

When I got into the magazine business there were no smart-phones, I didn't use e-mail, or even know what a double-click was, which all concerned me because the new business required the use of a computer. I figured out how to use the mouse, I got an e-mail address, and proceeded on to graphic design. Now I just had to figure out what a pixel was.

I knew nothing about computers or publishing, but I did know the community would support the project if I could figure out how to make it work. My product offered a value to consumers, businesses, and it included information that couldn't be found elsewhere in this coastal community. There was nothing like it around. It had to work!

I was running my "day business" as the Waxman the whole time I was learning to be a publisher. I worked all day and learned publishing software at night. No dates, no toys, no vacations, and no parties. It was a year of long hours, seven days a week. If you want results, be willing to lay the foundation, and always maintain cash flow while on new projects so the company can reinvest in itself.

I'm a creator as opposed to a maintainer so the best time I had was the first year. I made more mistakes that year than any five years of my life combined. I knew nothing about publishing which was what made it all so exciting. Getting immersed in something we know nothing about is how we grow and learn new things. It's also how we find out what we're good at.

I didn't get along well with computers. Once a neighbor came out at midnight asking if I was having computer problems as I was schoolin' mine with a sledge hammer. I convinced him that I had no anger issues. The computer deserved it. I also remember the day a pallet of magazines was delivered to my driveway and it started raining, hard! I didn't have a garage at the time and I never thought to invest in a tarp. Those were my "Good ole days."

Anyone could do it when there's a guide book. Building that magazine had no guide book, at least not for what I wanted it to become. I had to make it all up as I went. In a way, a standardized guide book was available because niche publications have been around for decades. It was no new idea, but following "the book" is what gets you the same thing everyone else has. I wanted something unique. I didn't know WHAT to think while putting that business together, but I knew HOW to think, which is what recreated the concept and ended up dominating its own industry.

I consulted with people in the printing business, which has an art to it. People consult for advice on what to do. I do the same, but there's also value in reading between the lines to find out what NOT to do.

I often saw a guy at business networking meetings who owned an advertising agency for over thirty years. Every day his staff was making cold-calls and looking for new business. Thirty years in the same business in the same town and still out looking for business every day!

The company claims to be experts in "marketing." Why do they not have prospective clients wrapped around the building with a six-month wait for their service? These people are easy to find. Talk to them, beg for advice, listen closely to every word, then go home and do the opposite of what they recommend.

Before opening the doors

I've never been one to settle for, "That's how everyone else does it," and the last thing I wanted was to be out looking for new business every day thirty years later. I knew the solution to this challenge would be to offer more value than competitors, which means doing things different than anyone else had ever done. I needed to reinvent every facet of the business. I faced wall after wall and wouldn't quit till each one came down. I broke up the company's tasks and made each as efficient as it could be before moving on, and found a way to improve every part of the business that made competitors look like they weren't even trying.

When it was time to try different desktop publishing software programs I found most to be difficult to navigate and time consuming. Who wrote some of this stuff? The various graphic programs I tried were very complex. A simple task that should only take a few minutes seemed to take hours. It wasn't my unfamiliarity with the software, it was how they were designed to work. It was as if code writers try so hard to prove how smart they are instead of making software efficient and user-friendly.

I was eventually accepted as part of the new digital generation, after all I had an e-mail address and everything. I thought I'd check out this thing called Google, (I heard everyone was doing it,) which is where I started my search for graphic software one would use to build a magazine. I tried several different desktop publishing programs and found one offered by a company in the UK. I downloaded a free trial version, used it for a couple days, and found myself on the phone every few hours asking questions, and sometimes telling them how I thought desktop software should work. (As if I knew what I was talking about.)

Thinking I was a nuisance, and perhaps on the edge of being booted from their system, I thanked the technical assistance staff and promised I'd stop calling so often. They commented on my call log history mentioning some of the specific items we discussed, and requested I do the opposite. The company was looking for people that knew little about desktop publishing to "partner" with by providing suggestions on how to make their software the most user friendly on the market. The deal was to help provide ideas that would create a unique desktop publishing software program, and in return you'd get reduced prices and/or free software.

If simplicity was what they were looking for, I was their guy! A lot of my suggestions got adopted. The finished product was desktop publishing software program that enabled me to work at least twice as efficient as anyone else in the business, and I got it for free.

Finding the right software was only one item of focus. What was really going on here, and what I think made it all work, is that I was facing every task of the business and making each as good as it could be before opening the doors. If you're not better, you're not different. And if you're not different, your percentage of the marketplace will always be minimal.

People embrace the phrase "Don't reinvent the wheel." But the wheel can always be made from materials more resistant to corrosion. It can be faster, lighter, more resistant to scratches, and you can always find a way to make a better one for less money. I looked for the multiple wheels that would be spinning the business and I reinvented each one of them. I reinvent the wheel every chance I get, and I think the phrase stops a lot of people from being just a little better than a competitor. A little is all you need.

There are rules when it comes to reinventing the wheel. Doing a tiny bit more and getting a lot more in return is what you're after. But be cautious of the opposite, which is doing a lot more for a tiny return. The trick to this is knowing when to say, "That's good enough," and start focusing on the next wheel. You also want to avoid doing what you want or like to do. Focus on what you NEED to be doing.

Surrender the Booty

After a couple years our popularity and readership grew and I wanted to send out a "ping" to see if anyone was listening. I created "Surrender the Booty," a scavenger hunt in the form of a treasure hunt. I used the magazine's pages to hide clues. If you could figure out the clues, you'd find a cooler of fishing tackle at the end of the trail. Hundreds of people were involved and it took three days for someone to finally figure out the clues, which were mathematical. They built a GPS number leading you to where I hid the key to a huge treasure chest.

The reason it went from a cooler of fishing tackle to a treasure chest is because word got out, people got excited, and donations in the form of prizes started coming in. That cooler of fishing tackle ended up being a chest containing thousands in prizes, winner take all! I'd say there were a few people following our magazine.

The treasure hunt was a way of creating exposure for our company, and ideas like that eventually made us so popular it released the burden of competition. Our competitive edge ended up being something competitors never understood. We had fans.

I was doing something most start-ups don't do; I was planning and positioning. Every day people go into business without an ounce of planning. People seem to plan their wedding more than their marriage. Don't be a statistic. If you're contemplating a business project, consider the "In-the-box" philosophy. Break your project up into multiple facets and make sure you know what you're getting into before proceeding forward. Create a list of things that will make people a fan of your business. If more people did this prior to starting a company, more would succeed.

There will always be surprises but planning as much as you can ahead of time will prevent some of them. Expect detours, and take them, but then get right back on track. Think of a plane leaving Miami headed for Dallas. Dozens of things can alter its course and original flight plan, and they do, but the plane still lands at its destination.

The UK software company was doing the same thing I was; perfecting each facet before launching. This can, and should, be done with any business. Saying "I'll just deal with it when I get there" can only take you so far. A dentist has years of preparation before he can stick his hands in your mouth, a police officer has months of preparation before going on patrol, and NASA puts years into preparation before launching, but when people want to start a business, they just jump right in and wonder why it didn't work out as planned. The reason is because it wasn't ever actually "planned."

Best Friends

By most, a friend is someone you can count on, learn from, grow with, forgive, stand beside, and someone you would support when they need you. And it goes both ways. One of the reasons businesses fail is because the owner doesn't build a relationship like this with their business.

As my magazine business started to profit a recession unfolded. I had never operated a business through a recession but it made sense to go right to work creating a plan that would take pressure off till the future was more certain. The new plan included selling things I didn't need at the time to loosen up cash flow. I also had a lot of free time and decided it wouldn't hurt to lock in a part-time job to ride out the recession. Profits from the company I was trying to save could now go untouched or reinvested.

I had not worked at a job in a while, so I was in for what I thought would be a refreshing change. The application process involved a lot of paperwork, time in a classroom environment, and a physical test. I was not in the best physical shape at the time, but I thought, "How tough could it be?" There were six parts to the physical test, and if you scored poor in one specific area you could use points from another to compensate.

The first test was on a treadmill while my vitals were

being monitored. I lasted about seven minutes before they had me start on the next exercise, which was range of motion. I failed across the board to the point of the staff wondering why I bothered showing up. The last task was upper body strength by doing push-ups. To pass the tests by trading points from one exercise to the others I had to complete twenty-eight push-ups.

From the push-up position I looked at the ground below knowing I had to do twenty-eight. It wasn't impossible, but I'd say it was not probable either. I had done more push-ups than that in the past, what I didn't realize was how far back in the past it was, and my faith meter was not exactly showing signs of life. If I failed I had to wait another six weeks before I could test again. Three strangers looked at a forty-year-old guy who only lasted seven minutes on a treadmill. Though I had done no push-ups yet I could feel pain in my arm from holding the ready-set-go position. I planned on doing what I could, stick my tail between my legs, and just get it over with.

I was angry at myself for not being more prepared and how I had let myself get into such poor physical shape. I had no excuse for it. I did one push-up and looked up at three hovering vultures waiting for me to die so they could divide up my personal possessions. They looked at each other with a grin thinking, "He'll never do it."

Pushing my body against gravity made me think of an astronaut breaking out of earth's atmosphere. Luckily for me, emotions were in play. I couldn't stop thinking about how I'd feel if I walked away a loser. After seven or eight push-ups, I knew if I could do three or four more I could at least leave with some dignity. My muscles failed around push-up number fifteen, but my heart took their place to compensate.

Like in the movie Rocky IV, when Stallone fought the big Russian, the once hostile crowd now cheered me on and encouraged me to keep going. Within a few minutes, the emotion of losing, combined with their encouragement, pumped out the required twenty-eight push-ups, plus I added a twenty-ninth so I could leave feeling like a champion as opposed to doing the minimum required.

What I took away from this; I was credited as the sole winner, but I didn't do it myself. Few people accomplish anything worthy alone. Others drove me through emotion, which is one of the most powerful things you can harness. If I were alone in that room I would not have done what I did. Emotions can work in your favor, and a negative emotion can sometimes be your best fuel. Here, self-anger was the motivating emotion.

My heart was more powerful than my triceps. If you put your heart into your challenges, people will notice. They'll also respect you, and support you, which will give you the strength to proceed forward. It's all tied together. It usually comes down to how bad you want something. I never did get the job, and it turned out I didn't need it. They said I was over-qualified, whatever that means. Apparently they didn't need someone who could do a lot of push-ups under pressure.

Being rejected for the job was a blessing. I was the publisher of a magazine with a lot of potential and I decided to put everything I had into saving it and getting it back on top. So my focus turned to keeping the magazine's head above water till the recession lifted. Competitors had deep pockets, years of experience, and most had a large company backing them. I didn't know where my new venture would end up because of what was happening economically, but I knew the community wanted this source of information, plus I had fans, something competitors lacked. Instinct told me to move forward.

While competitors were running scared, which leads to poor decisions, I remained calm and focused on creating a new plan. I needed to keep the magazine's heart beating for when the economy turned back upwards, but I didn't know if there would be enough profit for it to survive. Another question at this point is if it survives, do you want what it would become? I didn't want survival, I wanted to be the best.

I credit that recession for turning the magazine into an information source that dominated its own industry. The competitors I feared were not independently owned, they were divisions of bigger companies, and companies are made up of employees, and employees don't think like entrepreneurs. If they leaned back, I leaned forward. If they cut corners, I added corners. If they cut back on staff, I added staff. They cut back on content, I added content. When they dropped prices, I raised mine. I focused on doing the opposite of what competitors were doing.

History claims Walt Disney often did the opposite of what most people would do when he was in doubt. The philosophy was about how most people are wrong most of the time.

I can understand this philosophy. "Most" people, if they're honest about it, are not completely satisfied with their habits, finances, relationships or accomplishments, which are all a reflection of past decisions. So if you're not quite sure, do the opposite of what most people would do. It was risky but I applied this way of thinking to the company, and within a couple years all of my competition either gave up or tried to go digital. One competitor kept going but they must have had a separate source of income. The last time I looked they had four paid advertising accounts. At that time we had over a hundred.

Another challenge competitors dealt with daily was the cost of staff associated to advertising sales. I saw this long before I built the company, and I fixed that one too. I focused on information, they focused on selling advertisements. Our information attracted advertisers because the content caused more people to pick up the product. We maintained nearly one hundred percent of our advertising clients annually because our focus was on providing quality to the readership as opposed to selling advertising. This enabled a greater percentage of our client's money to go towards promoting their business.

The credit for that company's success had nothing to do with me being a talented publisher, nor did I have any gift or magic touch. Anyone could have done what I physically did. Competitors failed because they focused on doing things how they've always been done. The recession created a new game with new rules, and competitors didn't change to adopt the new rules quick enough to keep up.

Value is the secret ingredient that brings a business to life. And publishing, for me, was no different. Its core was about providing value. Its content was associated to boating and fishing and I saw a lot of fishermen attempt to compete with me over the years. They all made the same mistake, which was thinking their fishing and/or boating experience would help them at developing a competitive product.

I can assure you, boating and fishing has little to do with publishing a magazine about boating and fishing.

Hindsight tells me the business did so well because of three things; I had no experience, I did things different, and I built a relationship not only with the industry, but with the company itself. It trusted me to be there when it needed me, which was a two-way street. I was willing to do whatever it takes, I was willing to experiment, and I knew there's always a way. I understood how an obstacle like a recession may appear to be a coming nightmare and can turn out to be the best thing to ever cross your path.

A lot of people use lack of experience as an excuse to avoid starting their own business, yet having zero experience can be what makes a unique company. If you've been tempted by an idea but backed off because you didn't think you had the experience, reconsider it. You can teach yourself technical details along the way.

Lack of experience often creates unique ideas that end up changing the world, while knowing how everyone else does it leads to what the world already has. Past experience also turns me away from hiring people, I don't want them dragging bad habits called "experience" into my company. I don't hire degrees either, I hire integrity and character. If someone has that, together we'll find their skills, talents and gifts, and a place for those three to be woven into the company.

Identifying talents and finding a way to benefit from them is worth the effort. Bruce Springsteen is a well-known success, yet compared to the vocal gift within someone like Whitney Houston I wouldn't award Bruce for his voice. I would say the talent responsible for his success lies more with his ability to put his heart and soul into his music. Many vocalists have a great voice, but when Bruce sings, you can feel it. That's quite a gift. This may also be why most of today's entertainers are not consistently filling up arenas like Bruce and Whitney always could.

When you think you've exhausted everything you've got at your disposal, try using your heart. Zig Ziglar talked about a pole vaulter that was asked how he broke the world record. He said, "I just threw my heart over the pole, and my body followed."

No experience needed

The story of Ray Kroc taught us how we don't always have to be aware of our talents, nor do we have to be the first with an idea to make it work. Ray was known to be a guy that worked a respectable job, lived his life responsibly, and paid his bills. Ray provided for his family and home, like most working men at the time. In his early fifties he was thought of as an average hard working respected middle class American. He also had an undiscovered talent hidden within the layers of his character that may have never been known if not for one particular sales call. While trying to sell a milk shake mixing machine, he stumbled across a California based fast-food restaurant that had an unrealistic flow of customers. When Ray saw the crowds he developed a fantasy of duplicating their system in every town in America, and he decided to turn that from a fantasy to a goal.

Richard and Maurice McDonald owned an amazing high-speed fast-food machine on a street corner in San Bernardino, California. They didn't have much faith Ray could pull off the process of duplication, especially since their attempts to multiply the business had previously failed. But they were willing to at least listen.

As the story goes, Ray duplicated the business to prove he could make duplication work, but the brothers thought multiple restaurants would never work for long. They felt you would eventually lose the ability to maintain quality control. Ray's vision involved a lot of creative and risky out-of-the-box thinking, and he introduced ideas that had never been applied to a restaurant chain. He became increasingly frustrated with the lack of vision he felt the brothers displayed and decided the only way to proceed forward was to have control of the business all to himself. He sought out investors, bought out the McDonald brothers, and put his newly found talents to work. The rest, as they say, is history.

The McDonald brothers had the system, and Ray had the talent to create a near flawless duplication process. Combined, this had unlimited potential. Ray wanted growth and the brothers wanted quality, and if things were going to progress, something had to give.

Most people don't know this, but the McDonald brothers never got to enjoy the rewards of the billion-dollar franchise. Ray Kroc bought them out and left the McDonald brothers with a buy-out check and only their one restaurant in California. In time he made them remove the name from the building because they were not duplicating the McDonald's system, and within a few years it closed. From this point forward, the McDonald brothers were unassociated to the restaurant chain.

Before discovering McDonald's, Ray worked hard for the first fifty years of his life and he was happy. The second half was more exciting and motivating because he was working towards a vision, not just a paycheck. He was a dreamer but didn't know his talent would be in the duplication of a fast-food restaurant. Ray didn't know how good he was at franchising till he started one. He didn't know he was about to create a trend or go down in world history and have books written about him either.

You don't have to be first, you just have to be better. Google was a big hit long after AOL and Yahoo had the opportunity to take the lead. Google took things to the next level. These memorable names and companies, including Ray Kroc, took something that existed and expanded on it, proving you don't have to be first. I often wonder if it would have all worked had Ray been experienced.

The movie "The Founder" makes Ray Kroc out to be a shark. I don't buy that. I think that was Hollywood adding drama for ticket sales. If you find the story of McDonald's fascinating, look for the book "Grinding it Out."

The Three Kings
As time progressed the paper business did exactly what I planned; it put me out of a job. I wasn't retired by any means, I still had to work, but "work" in this case was a few hours a month. I was distracted by something I would have never expected to be a culprit; I had too much time on my hands. I got lazy and lost my creative edge. Life was easy and I let myself go mentally, physically and socially.

Studies show high "Like" counts on social media to trigger dopamine which we have yet to fully understand the long term effects of. As dopamine runs out, we go looking for more, creating an addiction. The desire to feel good is why most people can't put their phones down.

All of this creates distractions in our day causing us to get off-track. People think they need social media attention to feel wanted. You would think striving for a life that has few time restraints would be more inviting than trying to break our own record of how many "Likes" we get on a on a social media post. When responsibilities are neglected we somehow justify and blame, when the real problem lies with failing to do something worthy with our time.

I was distracted by boredom, and people have no idea how dangerous this can be. Countless studies have been done about how many things distract us in a day, and how much time it takes to reacquire our focus. One mentioned how the average person spends more than ninety minutes a day reacquiring focus. That's more than ten hours a week wasted, or five-hundred hours a year, on one thing. Five-hundred hours is a nice vacation!

There have been plenty of seminars and books written on the topic of time management, yet that phrase can clear a room quick. People don't want to deal with it. As society gets even more complex with portable computers and various distractions to keep up with, we're most likely only seeing the beginning of an era where time is redefined. I discovered the solution to time challenges and it doesn't take seminars, therapy or a stack of books; Do what you NEED to do first, then what you SHOULD be doing, then what you WANT to do. Of the thousands of "things" we all do in a day, you'd be surprised how many we want to, while what we should be doing gets neglected. This is the secret to creating time.

I blame our newly created fast-paced digital world on a lot of things, with lack of time on top of the list. Lack of time is similar to weight loss; people don't want to address it because they can't get results overnight. But if people could wave a wand and add three hours to their day, they wouldn't hesitate, yet that time would be also wasted, because they never changed habits which are what created the lack of time in the first place.

I found the secret to weight loss too. Most focus on two things; diet and exercise. Those are elements, not secrets. The secret is willpower. Focus on that and you'll be more likely to stick to diet and exercise.

Back to my boring life... I couldn't figure out what was bothering me so I hired a therapist. I didn't see what would be considered a problem but I wanted a second opinion. So I dumped my life on the table and said, "What do you see?" He said, "You're bored." I was expecting something a lot more exciting to be wrong with me. My goal building the magazine was to be bored. I customized it to specifically do just that. I saw how hard people work just to get by, I saw how little time they had for family and hobbies, and I wanted to develop a life that would offer free time. I did that, but I neglected to understand the need for a worthy reason to get up in the morning. To be truly happy you still need to be motivated and inspired by something you do.

Life was good, or so I thought. I was far from wealthy but bills were paid and I had a lot of free time to tinker with projects. Years ago I heard a business saying associated to three words; good, fast and cheap. The idea was that you could pick two. If it was cheap and good, you may not get it fast. If it was fast and cheap, it may not be good, etc. In life I use three words I refer to as The Three Kings; Time, money and significance. In this case, you need all three if you want a happy life. I took naps, went fishing, and didn't have a lot of responsibility, but something was missing. I was almost emotionally depressed because I wasn't doing anything to fill the need for significance, so I created a charity event through the paper's readership; The Fish36.

Fish36

The Nautical Mile monthly publication became a "go-to" source for the local marine industry and it offered resources I could use to create other projects. At the time this particular coastal community had about forty annual fishing tournaments as fund raisers for local charities. Tournaments are fun events offering fishermen a chance to compete and associate with each other. They've also proven to be great economic stimulators for coastal businesses like bait shops and marinas.

Almost every fishing event donated profits to a local cause, and even the winners often passed on their purse to the event's beneficiary. Because of my contacts and relationships in the coastal community, I was often asked to host one of these events. All I needed was a cause, then I heard about a kid's group looking to resupply their center with new toys and books.

Fishing tournaments were very "cookie-cutter." I wanted nothing to do with an event that had been duplicated so many times, and I wondered what would happen if I created a fishing event that catered to the non-fisherman. It had never been done in our area, it probably wouldn't work, people wouldn't understand it at first, and it had risks of not being supported. This had my name all over it! All I needed now was someone to tell me it couldn't be done. Within a few days I introduced and promoted the most innovative fishing event the coastal community had ever seen, the Fish36. I made a list of what needed to be done, resources and responsibilities, what needed the most focus, and I went to work.

My first job was to clearly understand what I wanted the end result to be. So many people move forward with an idea without knowing exactly where they're going, then find something to blame it on when they don't get there. If they knew where "there" was, the odds of getting "there" would be greater. My goal was for sponsors, donors and participants to look back afterwards and say, "Let's do it again." That would mean it all worked.

Maintaining focus is in capital letters on the top of my list of priorities. Everything else on the list will suffer if I'm not focused. I watch today's digital distractions prevent focus as people try to convince us how "multitasking" is a skill worth developing. I see it as a habit preventing people from producing a quality product. Your brain can only focus one-hundred percent. The more items you multitask, the more your one-hundred is divided, and items that require focus don't get the attention they need to function properly. Be human, get sidetracked, have fun, but at the same time, monitor your focus and stay on track.

I think about a scene in the movie Terminator-2 when I consider the importance of focus. The teenager Arnold Schwarzenegger's character was protecting began kicking and screaming because he wanted to do something to help his mom. The Terminator held him back and said, "This is not helping our mission." I think about that when I feel like I'm getting sidetracked on a project. Have fun, experiment, and sometimes an emotional fit is what you need to have an answer show itself, but know the goal and stay focused on actions that will ultimately contribute to the end result.

Most local fishing tournaments require a captain's meeting to discuss details and rules. Some teams showed up in matching shirts displaying their team spirit, but only one participant from each team needed to be present. This was usually on a Friday evening at a restaurant, and the next morning everyone would start fishing at sunrise. The targeted fish are usually the same three fish every time, and something called a "mystery fish" was usually included as an added bonus.

Your job as a participant of the event was to race around the local waterways as fast as you can looking to catch the largest fish you could find within a certain time. Officials were at the dock for inspection, who measured, weighed and released the fish back to the wild. Recognition went out to first, second and third place teams, and sponsors are categorized as gold, silver and bronze. Some tournaments may slide in something unique, but none deviated from the basic template.

My goal was to create something different. I first talked with tournament participants to find out what they liked and didn't like about tournaments. I also talked with tournament coordinators to learn of any unexpected challenges. Then I talked with fishermen that DID NOT take part in tournaments. If I could find out why, and what would attract them, I could increase the numbers. Then I talked with businesses known for sponsoring tournaments. This was a primary funding source, and I knew it could also be improved. I put it all in a bucket, shook it around one afternoon, and the Fish36 was scheduled.

I created a fishing event that attracted not only the active tournament professionals, but also the average non-fisherman who would normally avoid engaging in a competition. Based on participation, sponsorship donations, product donations, profit, and community interest, I created the most successful first-year event of its kind in the area.

It was considered a tournament by participants, but it wasn't a tournament by definition. There was no largest fish recognition, there was no first-place prize, and there were no trophies. I had people show up on a Friday afternoon to get a bucket. In the bucket was everything they needed. No meeting and no discussion. An event program displayed a list of thirty-six fish that could be caught in our local waters, and written instructions as to how this event works. The objective was to fish for the next thirty-six hours as you wish, targeting each of the thirty-six species. Catch one, and move on to the next. There was no particular order, and you were not expected to catch them all. It didn't matter how big a fish was, just take a photo and move on.

You could have multiple people on your team and you could split up and fish in different places. In the bucket were items associated to event sponsors that had to appear in your pictures to prove it was caught that weekend. Everyone was instructed to meet at a local marina thirty-six hours later to show us pictures of which fish their team caught.

At first it didn't seem very interesting to most, but that changed when people found out what they get in exchange for their pictures. Thirty-six hours into it all on a Sunday morning, people started showing up at a place we had been preparing for the past few hours. Participants walked into a decorated room that had almost $30,000 in raffle prizes spread out on tables, food from seven local restaurants, live music, and almost five hundred other people. Each raffle prize had its own ticket container and you could associate your tickets with what you wanted to win. Each qualifying fish picture earned ten raffle tickets. So if you caught thirteen different fish from the list, your team received one-hundred-thirty raffle tickets.

Some teams were one person, and some were a whole family. Each group that fished got to create a catchy team name and was assigned a team number. I attended other raffle events prior to planning this one to observe what worked and what didn't. One thing I noticed was a need to recreate the concept of calling out a raffle ticket number and having hundreds of people look through strips of tickets waiting for someone to raise their hand. This system took a long time and people got bored waiting, even at smaller events. Other event coordinators claimed, "people understand it takes time" and "that's how we've always done it" which are two big red flags in my book! I had hundreds of items and hundreds of people, it would take hours to give all of this away. Remember my goal; for people to want to do it again next year. If they have to wait hours in the heat to win prizes, would they come back next year? I had to reinvent the concept of a raffle.

Earlier I mentioned how people say, "This is how it's always been done," as opposed to the benefits of reinventing the wheel. Here we go!

I had a local printer run custom tickets with team numbers on them. So if you were participating on team number seven, all your raffle tickets were marked number seven. All you had to know or remember the whole day was the number seven. It was nice and simple. The tickets were not issued to individuals, they were issued to teams, and there were no restrictions to who or how many people could be on a team. If team number seven won a TV, the team had to decide who got it. So the fewer people on your team, the better you did with prizes.

We had eleven prize runners that volunteered from a local college fishing club. My job was to run around the room with a wireless microphone calling raffle ticket numbers. The custom ticket system we developed proved to be a big hit; the raffle moved along faster than volunteers could run prizes to the winners. We raffled several hundred prizes in just over two hours with no errors.

I needed a lot of raffle prizes to make this event a success, but that turned out to be one of the easier tasks. Businesses love donating something for a charitable local event if their name gets mentioned for the donation. I also needed to focus on sponsors which would cover event costs. Most fishing tournaments take months to gather a few thousand dollars in sponsorships. Even the events that are established have a hard time locking in sponsors every year.

A lot of events offer sponsors little more than a logo on a website. I once questioned a committee about what I think is a minimal return for sponsors. The feedback was, "It's all for a good cause," and sadly,

"What the sponsors don't know won't hurt them."
Sponsors pay the bills. They are the customer.
Sponsors and supporters are the reason there's food
on the tables at an event. They funded event
promotions, and this is how they're treated?

Character has been described as who you are and
what you do when nobody is watching, and results
are usually a reflection of your character. No wonder
it's so hard for events to get sponsors. If contributors
were treated with respect last year, it wouldn't be so
hard this year.

I decided if I was going to host this event, the
sponsors were going to get recognition, respect, and
results. I never discussed how our new event would
work with the public or prospective participants, I
didn't want anyone to have knowledge or details that
could lead to an advantage. I did, however, tell
sponsors everything. I created a list of what sponsors
would get in return for their donation, I offered more
of a return than they were used to getting, and I
explained in detail how the event was going to work. I
got $30,000 in sponsorship commitments literally
overnight.

Results like that usually get followed up with
comments of luck, then jealousy, then the inevitable
stack of excuses as to why I could make things
happen where others failed. I had been operating

with over a hundred companies in the coastal industry for years. Companies are owned and governed by people. As time passed, the people that ran those companies grew accustomed to me offering value in return for any business they did with me. I could have been selling rocks and they would have said yes, because they knew there was more to it. They were buying my credibility and reputation. Events that had a hard time getting sponsors spent their time spamming impersonal solicitation e-mails and never bothered building their reputation.

Signing up so many sponsors so fast was not because of my sexy phone voice, and it wasn't the event's popularity or past success, because the event didn't exist prior to this. It reflected the reputation I built in a business community. People knew that if I was involved, it was worth participating in. They also know if it completely failed, I would find a way to make it up to them or mail a full refund out of my own pocket. Plus, some things should be done in person. If people can't look into your eyes you lose the ability to communicate an emotion of trust. This has led to my philosophy on entrepreneurism; build the person first, then the enterprise.

You're not going to build relationships or a trusted name through apps on a phone, and few things offer more of a return than a trusted name. People may not know or understand the details of what you're offering, but if they trust you, you've at least got their attention.

I was advised not to create or host this event. I was told if there was no big prize for a winner, and if it wasn't done "tournament style" nobody would participate. Here again, "Don't tell me I can't do it!"

Many participants were known professional tournament goers, and they commented about how much they enjoyed this event in particular because there was no stress or pressure to win a first-place position. This was something they have their wife and kids involved with for a fun weekend on the water. Now that the wives saw how much fun fishing events could be, they were open to their husbands fishing more tournaments. (I scored some points with that one!)

The event was perfect for a local charity as an annual fund raiser. Now that the foundation was in place, sponsors were committed, and the details were worked out, my decision was to donate the event to a local charitable group, but I had no takers. It ended up being dissolved.

CHAPTER TEN

BACK TO SCHOOL

The next chapter of my life is what created the ingredients of what will be my next adventure, which is to develop an educational system based on the habits and behaviors of an entrepreneur. I'll be excited to read that one myself.

This door opened with comments from a friend in the Marines. I wanted to connect with America's younger generation and develop something that would help them adopt personal leadership skills. Connecting people with different generational beliefs can be quite a task. Other than fellow entrepreneurs, who better than a Marine to consult with when you want to find a way to do something others find to be challenging?

I had an interest in creating something educational I could introduce to high schools and possibly correctional facilities. High school students could use more than how to memorize enough information to pass a test, and many people in correctional facilities made a mistake. Some will be returning hours after release, but some only need a shot of hope to overcome whatever it was that got them into trouble.

I told my friend I was looking for something that would push me, I wanted it to be powerful, and I wanted it to have a positive impact on America's younger generation. I told him I was ready to dedicate the rest of my life to making it happen. He asked if I was willing to die for it? I was not sure I wanted to go quite that far, then he explained his question with, "If you can find something worth dying for, then you've also found something worth living for." I did find something worth living for.

Getting connected

Creating projects like fishing events and treasure hunts occupied my time and created temporary wins, but those quick wins we all look for often come with long term disadvantages. I see a lot of people jump from win to win and wonder why they're not happy. I wasn't unhappy, but something was missing. I was in search of that Third King; significance.

My first challenge was getting past how the publishing business caused me to be personally lazy. Life was easy. I lived on the tip of a fairly unpopulated island and didn't spend time with many people. I quit associating with other business owners, I gained a few pounds, and even lost interest in hobbies. I wasn't depressed, I was bored, and it was time to get back in the game. I didn't know which game I wanted to be in, but I knew it was time to find or create one.

I've always known networking with local business groups to have value. Being "connected" offers opportunities and associating with others in business helps maintain social skills. When you attend business luncheons or ribbon-cuttings you just never know who you'll meet or how being associated with them could benefit your goals, plus these groups usually have educational guest speakers.

Through a networking group I saw a promotion for an annual dinner hosted by an organization encouraging entrepreneurism. I attended, and it turned out to be an excellent example of how you just never know where something may lead. The event itself was disappointing. The host tried his best to be funny but it didn't work, and the speaker panel nearly put me to sleep. It was held, however, in a nice town on the beach, so after enjoying a beautiful sunset and getting some sand in my toes, I made the two hour drive home and accepted it as all part of getting back in the game.

The next morning I found a business card on my desk from the dinner that wouldn't end. It was from a high school teacher seated at my table. I overheard him mention how his school started an entrepreneur's class and they were looking for mentors.

This did not interest me. I never had kids and I didn't feel comfortable associating with younger people. I've always been nervous about how my business accomplishments as a high school drop-out may cause kids to think it's okay to quit school. At the same time, I was curious about what this involved, so I made the call. I explained my background, my lifestyle, and my past experiences, and this guy acted as if he discovered buried treasure. He asked if I would come to the school so I could have a look at the program and meet his students.

Every Wednesday
The class ran all year long and started with students breaking up into small groups. They form a fake company, invent a "widget," and spend the year putting it through the steps of a business plan. The goal is to present their project to a group made up of volunteers and teachers at the end of the school year. It wasn't exactly a "Shark Tank" opportunity, but if the project had possibilities students were invited to present at a local college.

It looked fun, kids were energized, and though it was a five hour round trip from my home I accepted the opportunity to be a weekly volunteer. My job was to come in every Wednesday for an hour and help students stay on track. Kids can easily scatter ideas into things that would never work. I'd keep them "grounded," and occasionally throw them a bone, yet allow them to be the ones who did the work.

Looking back, what drew me to the class was how mentors helped me learn so much about the real world as a kid, and the value it offered later in life. I saw this as a way to give something back.

What kept me motivated and energized all year was how much I was learning from teenagers and how their character and attitude was opposite of the stereotype society has given them. I'm sure there's plenty of exceptions, but the kids I got around were hard workers and very inspirational.

I found high school kids to be no different than adults; when we're in a group, we follow the "herd" and do some pretty dumb things. But in smaller groups or individually, we're all pretty smart.

As weeks passed I saw students lose interest in the class. Parts of the curriculum were very technical and complex. I agree the multiple facets of creating an enterprise need to be present in a program like this, but it needs to be fun too. If it's not fun, teenagers don't engage. I didn't like seeing this at first, but later saw it as a way to weed out students not serious about learning the depths of entrepreneurism.

The first year I volunteered was with a class of twenty-four students and I personally worked with a group of five. The teacher asked me to work with this specific group because they were several weeks into the project and still had no "widget."

This was a great business class, but I wouldn't exactly call it "entrepreneurism." It wouldn't have been appropriate to deviate from curriculum, but I could add flavor to it, so every Wednesday I'd spend a few minutes talking with the class about something entrepreneurial before we broke up into groups for the day. Some of the students I worked with still send thank-you notes about how those mini-talks helped later in life.

As I looked through curriculum I noticed there was no information about where ideas come from. This was a surprise since their first task was to create something from scratch. I was also surprised how creative thinking exercises were not required learning skills in an "entrepreneur's" program, so our first talk was about where fresh ideas came from.

This opened up an opportunity to communicate how companies gather staff attempting to "involve" employees by what they consider brainstorming ideas that could make the company more efficient. In this scenario, they gather on the same day of the week, with the same people, in the same room, at the same time, with the same ambient noises, in a room with the same smells looking at the same pictures on the walls. As people sit next to the same person they sat next to last week, the company asks them come up with new ideas.

Management actually puts that much SAME in a pile and complains when it doesn't turn into new ideas. This is one of the many problems with today's corporate thinking; managers were once an employee who did a job well and got promoted because of it. They still know how to do the job well, but doing that job well is no longer their job. Their job now is to manage others that do the job, and they were never taught how to do their new job, which was to manage. As production suffers, somehow blame falls on the employee's lack of commitment. It's amazing how many companies haven't figured this out.

Even worse, the brainstorming sessions were about the company, and nothing of interest to employees. If it's not a win/win you're most likely not going to get a lot of great input or creative ideas from employees.

When you're looking for productivity, it's important to evaluate what talents and skills you bring to the table and put them to work. The most value I could offer this high school class was to share what I learned from mentors in the form of skills that could be used later in their life. I saw sharing my experience in classrooms as an opportunity to teach kids things they could actually use in what I'd call "the real world" long after graduation.

One of our topics of conversation was about how you need to change your surroundings if you want to stimulate the creative side of your brain. This is what drives new ideas to the surface. What came to mind was how we go into a room and forget why we walked into it. The older you get the more often it happens. Some experience this several times a day. We think little of the occurrence as it happens, but hidden within lies the secret to fresh ideas. The brain restarts when it's exposed to a new environment which brings fresh ideas to the surface. This is why a company's Tuesday brainstorming sessions are not likely to end with fresh new ideas.

(If you stop and say why you're entering a room, like "keys," before you pass through a doorway, you'll remember why you entered the room.)

Since my group did not have a class project I took them out into the hall, sat them in a circle, and taught them how to brainstorm as a group. Within minutes ideas started to flow and we had a great project that could easily be put through a business plan. What they spent weeks on with no results only took minutes to fix as a group once they learned where ideas come from.

The widget from our brainstorming session didn't exactly have "teeth." I explained to the students how this was why they were weeks into the program and still didn't have a project on the table. The goal was to impress a group of investors at the end of the school year with something that could sell, while they were focused on having fun. We talked about the importance of setting sights on the goal, then working backwards to create a plan of action. We also talked about how life was full of compromises and sometimes you have to postpone the fun stuff to make things happen. I explained how fun and excitement will be part of the project, but if those are inserted in the wrong places, the project suffers.

Many adults are suffering because they put fun over priorities.

Other groups in the class had widgets that appeared to be more fun to work on, but those groups later got stuck on how to incorporate their product into the facets of a business plan. If that happens, you lose. The goal is to win. This was an example of something I see missing in society; people want things to be fun and exciting, and they want it now, with little consideration of what the end results may turn into. I talked with students about how there will be excitement, but in this case excitement doesn't come from the product, it comes from investors approving your financial request enabling the ability to proceed.

It also opened an opportunity to explain the benefits of delayed gratification.

I explained why we needed to first build a proper foundation in order to finalize a product that would meet the long term goal, and I was losing their attention. I was guilty of why the class was boring, so I explained how after the investors approve a loan they could use some of it to buy a sports car. Boom! They were focused again.

Even though this was an exercise with a fake product I wanted them to take it seriously so they would know how things would work in the real world. They never heard anyone talk like I did, and we were building a great working relationship. The students in my group trusted me and we moved forward.

I attended class every Wednesday to help with all of the groups, yet focused on my group of five. Months went by and it was time to start working on presentation skills. I'm big on presenting. I firmly believe what we get and how we're treated by others is a reflection of how we present ourselves. Whether you're dating, talking with co-workers, or getting pulled over for a traffic violation, you're constantly "presenting" yourself through life.

Surprisingly enough, presentation skills were not part of the curriculum. One day I had everyone go around the room and do a thirty second "elevator speech" on their project. They didn't know we were going to do this and I was randomly calling names to catch of them by surprise.

Everyone stumbled through their talk, then I had each do the same thing again. The second round went much better. I was demonstrating how if you practice just before you present, you'll remember more and you'll speak with more knowledge and confidence. Adding tips like this throughout the school year helped everyone do better on presentation day.

To me, that's a life-skill. If those kids can remember the benefit of a tip like that, the next time they're about to go on a job interview they'll be practicing instead of playing on their phone prior to the interview.

Some of the students didn't understand why I asked them to talk because they were not going to be the ones talking on presentation day. I asked what they planned on doing if their team leader was not present that day? Would you allow your whole team to go down the drain because you didn't have a back-up plan? If you're on a team it's important to know what others on the team are doing or at least what their responsibilities are. Being somewhat aware of what each is responsible for will create an unseen sense of accountability within the group.

This thought came from a talk I listened to by a guy who acquired wealth at a young age. He talked about how his decision to make money came from challenges in his childhood and how they led him to believe money would solve problems. He quickly became a millionaire but a year later he was broke and in debt. His saw the mistake to be a reflection of how he never learned about multiple facets of his business and had no idea what staff and employees were doing. This led to the company to spiraling out of control, and eventually out of business.

He regrouped, accepted responsibility for what happened, paid off debts, and went back into the same business. But this time he did something most claim to do but don't actually do; he applied what he learned from mistakes. He went on to be respected as the most successful person in his line of work. The most interesting part of this story is how it all happened between age seventeen and nineteen.

The end of the year rolled around and teachers gathered students into the school's auditorium for presentation day. The investor panel was not real investors, and there was no crowd in the seats. The only people in the room were volunteers and teachers on their lunch breaks sitting at a table in front of the stage. The plan was relatively simple; each group got fifteen minutes to introduce themselves, explain their role in the company they've created, and why the panelists should consider investing in their project. Eight months of work all comes together in fifteen minutes. That's why I pushed them so hard to learn presentation skills!

A few days prior to the big day I gave the class a pep talk about how there's always going to be "holes" in a presentation. When you're presenting and you step in those holes, or if things don't seem to be going well, express how you're passionate about your project. An investor often considers the person, or group of people, behind a product. And if that person or group has no passion for what they're doing, an investor may have second thoughts about writing a check.

That too should be considered at a job interview. Are you passionate about working with this company? Or do you just want a job?

My group entered the stage completely prepared to rock the house, to find the auditorium's computer system was not working. The available laptop was not sending a signal to the big-screen so they couldn't show a video we shot at the school a few days prior. Their project was something mechanical and fairly difficult to describe in words. The three-minute video offered a visual and completely changed your understanding as to what the product was designed to do. It was their "ace in the hole" and now they couldn't use it.

This was also the first time they experienced stage fright. People claim speaking to a group or crowd to be one of America's greatest fears, and programs like this offer the opportunity to have kids beat this fear at a young age. The fear of a stage combined with video equipment not working put them in a tough spot. I couldn't have asked for a better example of how the world demands results no matter how many surprises or challenges you encounter along the way. Those who throw their arms up and claim they couldn't because _____ will lose. You're not likely going to make excuses and money at the same time.

Knowing the goal was to present their project on a stage I requested to take the whole class into the auditorium weeks prior to presentation day. I wanted them to feel what it was like to stand on a stage and hold a microphone. I knew practicing in an empty two-thousand seat room would help them with stage fright. Many entry-level speakers tend to stare at a specific area or in a certain direction, so I wanted to show them tricks like panning the audience. The school saw no value in it and my request was denied. Needless to say, I developed quite a love/hate relationship with the "system."

Back on stage, the group I was personally working with all year remembered a recent talk in the classroom about what to do when you're backed into a corner; block the problem out of your head, along with any unnecessary distractions or noise, and focus on nothing but the goal. Look around, evaluate everything at your disposal, and find a way to make it work. I often think of James T. Kirk from Star Trek. He didn't believe in no-win scenarios. You may have to alter or create a new plan as you go, but there's always a way to win. Find it.

A student in my group realized he needed the judges to see what was on the laptop and the lack of being able to use the big-screen was in the way. He pulled cords out of the laptop and walked off the stage. He took it to the panelist's table and said, "Watch this video," then returned to the stage for the rest of the presentation, to find the microphones no longer worked. So they just spoke louder. Fourteen groups presented that day, and thirteen completely tanked. Watching that kind of ingenuity from a seventeen year old was inspiring. We're still in touch today.

(The following year the microphones and video system malfunctioned again.)

In class I watched kids get a passing grade yet never completed their work. Some hardly showed up at all. I was told if they didn't pass, parents would complain to the school, and it was just easier to give them a passing grade. Apparently this has been going on for quite some time. When I was a kid, if I didn't pass a class I was the one in trouble, not the teacher. I guess

I've been out of the loop with how things work.
In the sixties people knew how to get results from a protest. They had a justified reason to be upset, they came together, and they got results. Today it seems people are just mad at the world and lashing out. I've seen adults shift to the concept of complaining loud enough till someone gives them something just to shut them up. Just in case you were wondering where kids get their habits from....

A teacher's job is progressively becoming more about politics than it is teaching. Private conversations with them helped me develop a tremendous respect for both teachers and members of the school board. They're not only faced with today's current challenges, they also have to plan what tomorrow's challenges will be and the pressure of developing a plan for them too. Teachers and other staff within the system can't just do what they want, or what parents want, and they don't have a magic wand.

In the class I volunteered with I watched students begin with dreams of being the next great entrepreneur, and by the end of the year some were more interested in having a job in a factory. Hopefully as the class progresses it will understand how many advanced life skills are hidden within the layers of entrepreneurism and incorporate them into curriculum.

Role models

You don't have to look far to find someone saying, "Kids these days" in a negative way. We're flooded with complaints about their attitude and work habits, and I blame parents. Parents have been horrible role models for the last two or three decades. It's funny how you can't drive a car till you prove you know how, yet you can have kids and be a parent with no instruction at all. We have rules for soccer, insurance, chemicals, banking and sales tax, but when you want to be a parent, it's a free-for-all! People with no clue how to win are responsible for guiding people who will soon be in charge of the Nation's future.

If today is a result of yesterday, what will tomorrow look like based on what we're doing today?

We've taught kids that you get a trophy even if you come in last. This started with good intentions without consideration for what it could turn into. This can destroy how a kid feels because in their soul they know it wasn't earned. They were cheated. Not knowing any better, later in life they expect good things to happen because they showed up. It also stops people from pushing their limits of endurance to win because they'll get a trophy either way, so why try? We're seeing signs of how things like this have contributed to an entire generation of people with low self-esteem.

I see the "every kid gets a trophy" trend as a great example of how much we've become an "I want it now" society. I believe in its philosophy; if kids try, they should be rewarded. Trying leads to failing, and failing leads to improving. Improving leads to getting better, and getting better leads to winning. There you go; learning how to win. So yes, I believe they should get recognized for participating. I also agree with consequences if they didn't bother showing up at all. But I can't comply with rewarding everyone equally. There's a reason people want every kid to get a trophy, and the objective of this can be accomplished, but the way it's being done has high risk of making things worse later in life.

This leads to people going out into the real world and finding out they're not going to win at work, at relationships, or at anything else just because they participated. Then they go looking for someone to blame their failure on. It's an example of what happens when we don't consider long term effects.

I had someone argue this with me by using the Super Bowl as an example. When a team wins, everyone gets a ring, sometimes even the towel boy. This is a different kind of reward. This one is for participating in a team effort. When it's a competition structured around honoring who worked the hardest, and the last person crossing the finish line gets the same reward as the first, we'll have long term physiological effects. It causes people to go through life thinking all they have to do is show up to be rewarded. I dare anyone to deny this is happening!

What would the Olympics be like if everyone got rewarded equally just because they showed up to the event? What would America's military be like if everyone got promoted to General just because they showed up to roll call? What would happen to a company if all employees got free everything just because they showed up to work yet didn't have to produce? Bankrupt! Then everyone loses. That's the direction some are headed.

People complain how they want this, that, the other thing, plus free health care and shaded parking. Life is tough, and as people get personally weaker and more easily offended, some are actually going out into the world looking for things to complain about.

Look around, we have millions screaming, "Someone, anyone, please take care of me!" When they get what they've been crying for, productivity, at home and at work, doesn't change. Nothing is likely to change because what they're asking for couldn't possibly change their situation.

This came up in a high school class. It created exercises about how important it was to understand problem identification before going on to problem solving. Look around at today's protest groups. Most have little understanding of what they're protesting. They get mad at the first person who doesn't agree with them, causing even more anger.

Two hundred years ago America's pendulum was on the far side of tough. People earned or they didn't survive. Today seems to be the complete opposite. When you can get results by complaining loud enough instead of earning it, expect trouble. If you think I'm on a soapbox, you're right. But it's not about every kid getting a trophy, it's about how we must come together as a Nation and center that pendulum if we want good things to come out of the next century.

Why entrepreneurism?
I see answers to our greatest challenges hidden within the layers of entrepreneurism. If we extract business from entrepreneurism what we have left is the most advanced set of life-skills one could ever want. It's about problem solving, finding the truth, and focusing on goals. Entrepreneurs are hard workers, they don't let gossip run their life, and they put responsibility above desires.

We don't see video clips of Steve Jobs running an office or scheduling, and we don't watch interviews with Elon Musk talking about the newest version of an accounting software program. We hear about their struggles and challenges. We're attracted to how they learned to win and how they solve problems. We hear about how they face fears, break habits, and learn from mistakes. This is what attracts people to the entrepreneur and the concept of entrepreneurism. And this is what can help younger people evolve into productive adults.

The students I volunteered with got buried in spreadsheets and data bases for months and eventually some of them wanted nothing to do with going into business. If that's what I thought entrepreneurism was I'd want to work in a factory too!

If someone wants to go into business I encourage them to learn things like tax laws, trademarks, banking, accounting, and the structure of a business. Now when lawyers are lawyering, and accountants are accounting, bankers are banking and managers are managing, you'll know what they're doing with your money. To clean that up a bit; allow others to do their jobs, but know what they're doing. Monitor progress without micro-managing. This will create a sense of teamwork and allow more time for creativity. This is the difference between working IN your business or working ON your business.

Associating with younger people opened my eyes to a big problem being dumped in their laps. While society points fingers in multiple directions, mine are being pointed at adults. We've allowed our character and habits to deteriorate, and it's rubbed off on the next generation. Adults have gotten consumed with their own interests. They're more interested in looking good socially and politically than they are in breaking bad habits and improving themselves. I see adults make time for a shot of dopamine from a social media post but claim to have little or no time to spend with their kids.

Younger people watch how when we can't figure out how to communicate, because it takes work, we just get a divorce. They watch how we jump on charitable causes, as long as it's convenient and doesn't interfere with vacation plans. And they watch us use credit cards putting our family into debt as opposed to saving for things we want. If you really want to know what's wrong with "kids today," look no further than their recent role models.

Adults have lost knowing what it takes to make things happen, they settle for "that's good enough," and kids learn by example. I'm convinced there are multiple factors responsible for today's challenges, and I'm also convinced younger people have few quality role models to learn from. But that's not the greatest problem. The greatest problem is where we will be in fifty years if this doesn't change?
Kids need role models. Be that, and we all win.

Bridging the gap

When I was in classrooms I wasn't a cop, a teacher, or a parent, so kids opened up to me. We "connected," and I found them to see more than adults give them credit for. Kids see how computers have altered the course of the world for the good, and how they've also disconnected us as people.

"Connecting" with high school kids was an interesting process. As a society we have little experience with this. People didn't live long enough to understand its challenges till recently. What took decades or even a century to evolve now happens in a few years. In the past someone forty years of age could talk with some eighty and understand each other. Today we have twenty-year old people teaching things to thirty-year olds, and that gap is tightening every day.

Years ago a sixty-year old person could say, "It's okay with me, I'll be dead and I won't have to deal with it." Today that doesn't apply. That thing you're not looking forward to, like banks closing and replacing tellers with touch screens, is not "evolving" over the next couple decades. It's happening now. Even our language is changing faster than we can keep up. Cursive is gone and texting with emojis and abbreviations is in. Over lunch a police officer friend was recently telling me he needed a written statement from a nineteen-year old and how he

couldn't understand parts of it. It was written with abbreviations as if it were a text message.
The winds of change are blowing. You better be checking for holes in your sails!

As I engaged with high school students I began to understand our social and economic society through their eyes, and how they see themselves eventually weaving into it. Younger people see how we've lost the ability to personally communicate, how we treat each other, and our inability to read body language or express emotion. They see how everyone wants to save the world yet they show little interest in saving themselves by breaking habits, beating fears or working harder. They see how people have lost the desire to personally accomplish and how we actually set goals to "get by."

I see more and more people settling for basic survival than ever, and kids see it too.

For those who remember copy machines; when we copied a copy it deteriorated and a copy of a copy of a copy was eventually so blurry we couldn't read it. I see this happening to our society. Each decade we lose a bit more respect, responsibility, and manners, and it's time to quit complaining and start putting solutions on the table. This can be done by teaching younger people entrepreneurial characteristics.

Kids see how our system does not teach how to win, it teaches how to survive with the "herd." They see our corrupt world of business and politics, and they're scared if they go to work in that system they're likely to be a statistic. They don't want to turn 65 dead from stress, lonely, broke, still working to pay for life's basic necessities and/or dependent on government or charity.

Sadly, these are categories most people fall into after working hard for thirty or forty years!

What I remember the most from spending time with high school kids is a conversation we had where I was looked at as some rock-star business tycoon. I explained how I didn't have buckets of money buried in my yard, I didn't drive a Bugatti nor did I have a vacation home in Switzerland. I was just a local guy with a small business that provided enough free time for me to come help out. One of the kids said, "You don't get it do you?" He said, "It's your character we want. Without that we'll never have the cars, the buckets of money or the overseas vacation home. While the course was about business tactics, I brought the need of developing habits and behaviors to the table. They were the ones who "got it."

I don't see younger people as stupid or lazy. I see them as scared, and in desperate need of guidance and mentorship.

Experiences in our youth teach us to go "by the book," and that information has its place, but life doesn't throw books at you. It throws surprises. Younger people tell me they see this, and they don't want to work hard most of their life ending up desperate in their old age because they never learned how to win. They want to create, build, and grow, but they also feel if they go out into the economic system being passed down to them, odds of ever reaching their dreams are slim.

Adults care, I'm convinced of that. But I'm also convinced they have no idea what to do about it. I do. Have kids study what makes an entrepreneur. Encourage them to study business if you like, but have them focus more on things that make up an entrepreneur's traits, habits and personal character.

There's a new phrase we're starting to hear, the "intrapreneur." This is looked at as the act of thinking like an entrepreneur but applying the habits and behaviors to a career path as opposed to creating an enterprise. Since less than ten percent of America's population is self-employed, this concept could develop valuable "in-house" problem solvers and alter the course of our nation for the good.

I volunteered one more year in the same high school then started writing my own curriculum for a private intrapreneurship skills class. I've made detailed business a small percentage of the program. The focus is on what an entrepreneur thinks as opposed to what one does.

What triggered this was a teacher telling me how a student from years prior developed a product that was a big hit and currently available in stores. Hundreds of kids attended this class in the past few years and only one was remembered. That ratio could be improved if more focus was put on what makes the entrepreneur psychologically and characteristically.

Looking back it's hard to believe all of that, and what is being developed because of it, came from going to a disappointing business networking dinner.

As we merge more into a world of digital connections as opposed to personally interacting, groups and clubs are starting to disappear. You don't "feel" when you're not live and in person. Sometimes I'd prefer to live in a cave myself, but if you join some networking groups you never know who you'll meet or where it can lead.

JIM GRIFFITHS

CHAPTER ELEVEN

DISASTERS

Hidden between projects lie my disasters. One could only imagine what I was thinking at the time, and I couldn't possibly remember them all. If I had to credit one thing that made any of my successes possible, it was the disasters.

I often think about how our connection to social media and portable computers will play out in the future. The more we disconnect from each other physically the more social skills fade, and eventually we lose confidence in ourselves.

In person we have to be accountable to what we say and do without glass to hide behind. I see this leading to less attempts at success because we're scared of what people will think of our failures. If we fail on social media, we can delete the post and it's forgotten in seconds. If we fail in person, everyone saw and remembers it forever.

Musicians and actors have piles more failed movies and songs than they do hits. Ball players have more missed shots, and pro fishermen retrieve more lures without a fish than they do with one. Instead of just looking at these people as successes, have a look at how their failures are what created their wins.

Computers and portable devices are relatively new to the world. We've yet to understand what it will do to people personally. As we all enter the world of being digitally connected be sure you're willing to do some of the dumb things that have a risk of embarrassment or failure.

Go fail at a few things. Failures are known to create some pretty impressive people, and failures are what make successes.

CHAPTER TWELVE

MY DOG BO

In 2004 I crossed paths with a dog (photo on the back cover) that became homeless during Hurricane Charlie. He wandered into a woman's life that couldn't keep him, and the local pet shelters had their hands full with other lost animals. At first we didn't connect, he was scared and didn't know where he was. But after a few minutes he was in my lap and we were buddies. I had no intention to keep him; the plan was to either find his owners or hold him till someone was willing to adopt.

I brought him home to a rental apartment I was living in at the time. The next day I went to work hoping he would be okay by himself for a few hours. When I got home I slowly opened the door to peek in and see how he did. The first thing I saw was a pile of shoes in the middle of the floor, my shoes. He was hiding in the bedroom and the shoes were undamaged.

As our relationship grew, he developed a habit of going straight for my shoes and then my socks when I got home. The only thing I could figure through the years was that he associated shoes to us being apart. When I put shoes on he would try to take them off, and when I came home, if I took my shoes off, it meant I was staying in.

If his previous owners were looking for him their first actions would be to contact local animal shelters. It would have saddened me to get that call, but it never happened. At this time if they were not looking for him, he would be staying right here with me. I had him checked out by a vet, got all his shots up to date, and we were a couple.

I named him Bocephus, after Burt Reynolds in the movie Smokey and the Bandit, Bo for short. Bo and I did everything together and our relationship grew into something I never expected. For me there was more to it. I had been a runaway, I didn't have a lot of friends, and I never had a relationship I would allow to grow. I was scared to let anyone get close to me, though it's possible this was more about me getting close to them.

The relationship I developed with Bo taught me to love, and how to be loved. It was my first time being responsible for something with a heartbeat and a pulse. I put his needs before mine, and when he needed something I took care of it. It was mutual. I think he did a lot more for me than I did for him.

When I later met my wife, I feared being close to a woman. I had a history of allowing a relationship to get to a point, and run away from it. This time things felt different. We talked a lot and she helped me overcome fears I didn't even know existed.

Not only was this woman everything I ever dreamed about, but she saw that I was on the edge of being able to break old habits and I had hope. I still had a lot of work to do if I was to become a great half to a human relationship, but hope and direction, along with someone that believes in you, goes a long way.

I'm convinced that had I not cultivated the relationship with Bo, I would not have had the ability to maintain a quality relationship like the one I have with my wife.

Bo was as healthy as a dog could be. He didn't have to see a vet outside of annual check-ups his whole life, then developed cancer in his mouth at the age of fifteen. That's old for a fifty-pound lab mix, but he was still chasing squirrels at that age. My wife and I agreed to do whatever it took to make his life as painless and enjoyable as possible, while also knowing his days were numbered.

We did everything available in the form of cancer treatment. Within about a year tumors appeared and one in his throat prevented him from swallowing food. In his condition he was not likely to survive the surgery he needed, so we had to do the unimaginable. I held him in my arms as he went to sleep, telling him that he didn't do anything wrong, and I said good bye to my best friend. As he fell asleep I looked over at my wife and realized how it was my relationship with him that made our marriage possible.

I published a pair of kid's books in memory of Bo under the name "My Dog Bo". I wrote one story of him going fishing with Sammy, our neighbor's pet. We also have a Doberman (Tiberius) and I wanted to include Ti in a book, so I wrote a second story and published another book about Bo getting lost while chasing a squirrel. Ti went looking for him. I hired a great cartoonist and sold a few, but sales were not the focus. It was about the memory.

I made a large flip-book version that I used at daycare centers where I would read to groups of kids, and parents still tell me it's their kid's first pick for a bedtime story.

I wanted to include Bo in this book because one of the things I learned from the relationship we built applies to why so many people don't get what they want out of life. I was scared to get close to anyone because of experiences in my childhood. I didn't think of myself as being in denial, I was simply unaware the fear existed. Bo offered the gift of discovering a world I never thought I could live in. He showed me how to love, something I was unknowingly afraid of.

Almost everyone has a hidden fear they avoid or hide from. Some have several. You'd be surprised what may be around the next corner if you can figure what they are, how they developed, and create a way to face, beat, or incorporate them into your life.

For those interested in truly exploring the world of entrepreneurism I leave you this; the act of entrepreneurism is associated to the act of business, but the entrepreneur is a person. Build a stronger person and you'll build a stronger enterprise.

JIM GRIFFITHS

"Break old habits and read lots of books. Study people that left bread trails, and direct your attention and efforts towards what you can be, not what you can get."

- *Jim Griffiths*

ABOUT THE AUTHOR

Jim Griffiths spends time with schools and business groups sharing the depths and multiple layers of entrepreneurism and the importance of developing the person before you develop the enterprise.

His goal is to introduce a curriculum available not only to the public and in schools, but also as a class in correctional facilities nationwide involving the characteristics and habits of an entrepreneur. www.TheThirdDraft.org®

Jim is available as a guest speaker for schools, colleges and business organizations.

He can be contacted through:
www.TheGriffithsGroup.com

(The Third Draft® is a registered trademark)

JIM GRIFFITHS

DON'T TELL ME I CAN'T DO IT!

www.ingramcontent.com/pod-product-compliance
Lightning Source LLC
Chambersburg PA
CBHW060027210326
41520CB00009B/1025